WHISPERS
FROM THE
CROSS

Reclaiming the Church
Through Personal Holiness

WHISPERS

FROM THE

CROSS

By Anne, a lay apostle

ISBN: 978-1-935566-81-6

Library of Congress Number: applied for

© Copyright 2011 Direction for Our Times

Publisher: Direction for Our Times
                9000 West 81st Street
                Justice, Illinois 60458

                708-496-9300
                www.directionforourtimes.org

Direction for Our Times is a 501(c)(3) tax-exempt organization.

Manufactured in the United States of America.

Graphic design and stained glass art by:
                Chris Deschaine
                www.braintrustdesign.com

How to Pray the Rosary information, is used with permission. Copyright © Congregation of Marians of the Immaculate Conception, Stockbridge, MA 01263. www.marian.org.

Copy of the painting of Madonna del Miracolo reproduced with permission from the Church of Sant' Andrea delle Fratte, Rome.

Painting of *Jesus Christ the Returning King* by Janusz Antosz

V11.11

Direction for Our Times wishes to manifest its complete obedience and submission of mind and heart to the final and definitive judgment of the Magisterium of the Catholic Church and the local Ordinary regarding the supernatural character of the messages received by Anne, a lay apostle.

In this spirit, the messages of Anne, a lay apostle, have been submitted to her bishop, Most Reverend Leo O'Reilly, Bishop of Kilmore, Ireland, and to the Vatican Congregation for the Doctrine of the Faith for formal examination. In the meantime Bishop O'Reilly has given permission for their publication.

Table of Contents

Whispers from the Cross

October 21, 2011

Every lover of Jesus Christ will eventually find his way to the foot of the cross, where he will gaze at the Crucified One and engage in contemplation of those wounds which delivered salvation to humanity. Through contemplation of these wounds, we find our own place in the salvation story. Our sufferings begin to become understandable as also co-redemptive, like Mary's, and therefore also meaningful and valuable.

Jesus gazes down at us from the throne of His earthly Kingship, that is, His cross, and He offers each follower His gratitude. Just as one views those rare friends who arrive to share suffering, Jesus views us, imperfect but present, lacking in full understanding, yes, but also tremulously interested and engaged in the pain of the Savior we seek to know and emulate.

Jesus saw His mother at the foot of the cross and He saw one of His twelve apostles, John. What qualified John to stand as both sentinel and witness to the most pivotal moment in the history of the redemption of mankind? Love qualified John and ultimately love will qualify each one of us, the apostles for this time. John was known as John the Beloved and it was love that allowed John to be intricately woven into the tapestry of the Passion.

Because John was present to Jesus at the foot of the cross, John witnessed the Savior's pain as Jesus asked, "My God, My God, why have you forsaken Me?" John learned about holiness through this experience of apparent abandonment and John also received His instruction which was "Son, behold thy mother."

So John, through love, later knew that feelings of utter abandonment were part of the experience of one who is commissioned to spread the Good News. And this made him strong. And John, through love, was able to execute the plan of heaven because he received his instruction directly from Jesus, which was to protect Our Lady and her role in the early Church. And this made John fearless.

In the same way, Jesus wants to teach us about those sufferings which will happen upon us as we make our way through our life's witness to God. In the New Testament, we find apostles willing and even eager to be crucified like Christ. This cannot be ignored. The model sent to us by the Father, of the Son, provides us with all that we need to successfully navigate the call to holiness that is love's mandate.

These whispers from the cross are our nourishment, our comfort, our balm and our portion. Whispers from the cross will direct us and correct us. These divine emanations from our Crucified King will console us and give us courage. Indeed even in the most humanly ridiculous circumstances of suffering and pain we will feel strength because we arrive daily at the foot of the Cross to receive and then offer what is Jesus instead of what is our feeble and changeable humanity.

Imagine Jesus whispering from the cross statements of love and tenderness, such as, "Thank you for being interested in My suffering." "I understand your pain." "Don't be afraid." "Trust Me to protect you." "Be about My Father's business." "Behold your mother." "Rely on Me." "Do not leave Me." "You are of infinite value to Me, just as you are." "I am with you." "I want to heal you." "I need your help."

Imagine Jesus whispering from the cross instructions on how to love those around us such as "Be patient with your spouse." "Be gentle with your children." "Be loving to My children." "Clothe the naked." "Feed the hungry." "Comfort the broken-hearted." "Feed My sheep." And, "Tell God's children about their Father."

Imagine Jesus whispering from the cross instructions on how to advance in holiness such as, "Be strong in the face of this temptation." "Be faithful to your vocation." "Decide against that which leads you away from Me and walk with determination into that which leads you closer to heaven in thought, word and action."

Jesus urges us to integrity and authenticity. Jesus, from the cross, shows us who we were created to become and urges us not to conform to the expectations of others but to the expectations of the Creator who created us to claim with determination our true, unique identity in Christ. Yes, our unrepeatable personhood can only be achieved and celebrated through contemplation of the Crucified Christ.

Apostles, do we want to be free? Do we want to be completely ourselves, fulfilling every promise that the Creator placed in us when He brought us into the knowing of His mind? Only by contemplating the humanity of Jesus Christ will we be able to fully achieve our own humanity. He is the first, the most complete and the highest possible example of how to live life as a created person of an all-loving God.

Apostles, do not think that our humanity is an obstacle to that which we seek in terms of transformation. Our humanity is the delight of the Creator and in our humanity is the promise of the Good News being carried to every person on earth during the time in which we have been placed, meaning, our time . True, it is only by being born into eternity, through death, that we will fully understand the promise of our individual being, but we will one day, "go forth in glory from the anguish and pain, in one moment to close the eyes that looked on the world of men and in the next to open them at once to look on God and Christ! The speed of this joyous departure!" (Callistus I, Pope and Martyr, *The Liturgy of the Hours According to the Roman Rite*).

Yes, the sublime truth is that we will one day close our eyes upon this world and instantaneously open them in the next, but until that moment, ordained by heaven, we must serve God on earth. In studying the Passion, we will come to understand how.

We gaze at the figure of Christ on the cross and we often contemplate a still form. Apostles, to fully engage in the humanity of Christ, we must picture Him alive. Study Christ on the cross in the three hours of His anguish. This study will bear fruit because in these hours Jesus suffered every temptation which can be presented to us by the enemy. Triumph came in the overcoming of these temptations. Victory was secured by going through the Passion. Victory would not have been secured by avoiding the reality of the Passion and if it was this way for Jesus then it must be this way for us.

Jesus was tempted to believe that His suffering would be in vain, wasted as it were, by man's rejection of Him and, by extension, the Father and all of the children created by the Father. This was not true. While many reject God, many choose God and embrace their share of suffering along with Christ. The question asked by Jesus from the cross is this: "What will you do? Where will you stand?"

Will you condemn Jesus, like Pilate, through terrible ambivalence and becoming lukewarm? Will you betray Jesus, like Judas, through rebellion and envy? Will you deny Jesus, like Peter, through fear and lack of conviction? Or will you remain with Jesus, like John, through a decision to love that is steadfast and constant?

The whispers from the cross that we experience in contemplative prayer are the beginning of intimacy which will be completely realized in heaven, even as it is introduced to us here on earth. This intimacy with the Savior provides nutrients for the seeds of virtue sown into our souls by the Father who created us.

The pain of Jesus separated from the sinner will remain as long as humanity continues on earth. By studying the Passion, we enter into this pain of separation with Him and we become filled with zeal to bring others to Jesus through the witness of our life and through any commitments God entrusts to us in the spreading of the Good News. The relationship with the Redeemer and each person is unrepeatable and irreplaceable and that is why Jesus grieves for every person separated from Him through sin.

Truly, Jesus wants to live His resurrected life in each one of us. It is sin which interrupts this presence of Christ within. Sin is actually a rejection of the union. Sin is deep ingratitude to Jesus for the gift of redemption. If we study the Crucified Christ, we learn that Christ absorbed all sin. Instead of returning hostility, Christ returned love. He offered love in His humanity, He offered love in His Passion and death, and then He rose from the dead and offered the exact same thing…love.

In accepting the reality of the resurrected Christ we have the formula for successful integration of our humanity with God's divinity. That is why Scripture tell us that we can only get to the Father through the Son. Imagine the early apostles trying to promote that message to an Old Testament people.

We study the cross because in doing so we allow the gratitude we feel to increase and we are then less and less likely to offer the ingratitude of sin to the Father as a return on the gift of His only Son.

Our indifference, our malice and our sin does not change the gift, of course. The gift remains the same and when we are willing to repent, we are willing to accept the gift. And that is our contribution, after all, the decision to accept or reject the gift that God offers through Jesus, meaning our personal redemption.

Dear apostles, we must give Jesus some time each day, silently contemplating His form on the cross and allowing Him to whisper intimately into our souls all that we need so that He can live in us.

Whispers from the Cross

Locutions

January 10, 2010
Jesus

All of time directs to the present and when God's children enter eternity they will enter timelessness. This concept of the eternal present is difficult for humanity to grasp until they are fully embraced by eternity. This should not cause distress to My apostles. The knowledge you will gain upon your death will be yours for eternity. It is better that you reconcile yourself to a limited understanding, even while you rejoice in the depth of the understanding that you do possess. Examine what I have shared with you and direct each action in each day toward the truths that you have been given. Scripture provides you with ongoing illumination and the Spirit, which never tires of teaching, flows in and out of the writings of Scripture in the same way that your breath flows in and out of your body. For as long as you live, the breath of life will flow in and then out, in and then out. See that Holy Scripture prompts the same action. The Spirit flows in and out, and then in and out, never pausing, never exhausting the commitment of God to His children on earth. I want My apostles to search tirelessly for truth but I want them to search in the places I have designated as places where truth will be found. Dearest apostles, so beloved to Me, please give Me all that you are. If you do not hold back from Me, I will be able to give you all that I am. I want to do this. I want to be consuming for you so that you will be consumed by the peace that I bring to our

11

relationship. Do not strike out on a private search, away from the faith that I have brought you to. Come further instead into the truths that I have given to the Church entrusted to Peter, the first Pope.

January 11, 2010
Jesus

Dear apostles, so often I have counseled you to see yourself as small so that I can be seen as God in all of My power. I repeat this plea today. I know that My apostles love Me. I know that you wish to serve Me and I see your great efforts toward the work I have entrusted to you. And yet, many of you continue to take the assignments I have given to you and impose your will on them. Do not be confused. I see that you are serving Me and trying to do My will. What I am asking you now is that you give greater consideration to completing your work for Me, My way, not your way. My way is different than your way. My way is to advance into each day's work in complete humility and complete willingness. I was a victim to the Father's work. I ask that you, too, be prepared to be a victim to the Father's work. Only in this way will we, together, be able to draw people back to love and then from there to service. Beloved ones, you will be disappointed if you look back and see a lifetime of service to Me done with the spirit of selfish humanity. You will be so sad and so remorseful. Will you be welcome in My kingdom? Of course you will be welcome home. But you will feel much more joy upon your arrival if you rebuked your temptations to be seen as important and powerful and, instead, embraced My Spirit of humility and selflessness in your service. People are drawn to Me because I am kind and because I love them. They know that I forget their past mistakes and sins. They are safe with Me and they can rely on compassion from Me. They should feel the same way about you. Do they? Later, people, in their journey through life, become afraid and anxious and then they rest in My power and My power is there for them to keep them safe. But first comes love. Be humble in your work, dear apostles. Conduct yourself like the King, who is served because He is loved, not because He is powerful.

January 12, 2010
Jesus

My beloved apostles, your service is so important to Me. Together, we prepare the world for My return. There is no time to waste because there are a certain amount of tasks assigned to you each day. If, on any given day, you decide that you will reject My will, that day's work is left undone. Which day can you examine and say, "Jesus did not use me today." There are no days like that. I use you each day in ways that you do not understand. All I require is your willingness to be used for the good of the Kingdom. If you are willing, I will use your service, your suffering, your decision to proceed in your work despite any uncertainty you feel. All is utilized for the good of souls. I see that you desire to serve Me and that is why I am giving you these words. You have served Me in the past and you desire to serve me today and on into the future. And yet, you are suffering and you are uncertain. My dear apostle, if you will accept that I, Jesus Christ, have made the decisions about your work and the graces I will flow through your work, you can serve with greater peace. If you are willing, the rest is left to Me, not you. There is no need to spend a great deal of time worrying and wondering. Remain in the day's work and know that if I want you to change your course, I will make it very clear to you. Otherwise, continue on in the service in which you find yourself. Think back on the times in your life when you experienced My call. You knew you were being called. You felt peace about the direction you were taking for Me. Well, I am still with you. I am with you right now. I assure you, if I want you to know something about your work, I will communicate it to you. Be at peace. I am the director of the Renewal. You are a servant to the Renewal.

January 13, 2010
Jesus

I am present in the events that occur in the world. All that occurs will ultimately help My children to choose good over evil. Be assured that I do not abandon humanity. My dear apostles, there are times when you find life difficult or when you feel afraid. This is inevitable and I have given guidance for you to cross these periods safely. You must expect this, of course. But I tell you that some people keep their peace during even the most trying times and some people lose their peace during relatively easier periods. Why is this? Perhaps my dearest apostles should expect difficulties and trials. Perhaps it is time for those serving Me to consider that persecution and distortion spoken against one is the experience of the follower of this time. It has always been this way and that is true, but this historical period of time in which you are serving will include more of this experience rather than less of this experience. If my beloved apostles expect this treatment and accept it as an inevitable part of their service to Me, they will have an easier time retaining peace throughout the trials to come. Please, dear apostles, do not compare your experience to others. Do not be one who wishes he could serve in another life because the other life appears less taxing. Crosses come to all apostles and if you are carrying a heavy cross now, so be it. That means that this cross belonged to this day for you. I want you to retain your peace and I will help you but remember this. When I carried My heavy cross during the cruelest persecution, My suffering was evident on My face. I could not hide it. You will, at times, appear to be suffering and you should not feel you are failing because you need help or because your suffering is evident to others. If you call out to Me throughout your suffering and if you accept the help that I send gracefully, you will have peace. I will give you a share of the dignity that accompanied Me through My Passion.

January 14, 2010
Jesus

My beloved apostles share in My dignity, it is true. By dignity, I do not mean comfort. I was not always comfortable, least of all when I was carrying the cross that redeemed mankind. Throughout My Passion, though, I possessed the dignity that belongs to a child of God. All of mankind possess this dignity and nobody can take it from them. Followers of Mine will look out at the world from their soul, united to Me, and they will desire that each person be treated as I would like them to be treated. Followers of Mine will hear My anguish at the mistreatment of so many. Beloved apostles so close to My heart, hear Me. Listen to My pleading. There is a heavenly answer for the suffering of many and a great deal that My children suffer is unnecessary. Look at your own life and think of one instance where you helped another. You diminished the suffering of one of God's children in that instance and lightened their cross, lessened their loneliness or provided some physical assistance that I wished this other person to be given. I used you to bring My loving kindness to this other person. I used you to affirm their dignity. How many of you are there? How many follow Me? May I say that if you were all listening to My voice, serving as I would like you to serve, I could bring more comforts to many more of God's children. It hampers My plan when people chosen to serve refuse to serve as I wish them to serve. Sometimes, I have to remove someone from service all together in order to protect God's children. Imagine the grief this causes Me. Not only do I feel the gap in service, but I have to mitigate the damage that has been done by the false representation of Me. Others must work harder in these circumstances and others suffer. Perhaps you have suffered from the false representation of another. Your crown will reflect this, have no fear. Your reward will be great. For now, serve on, conscious of the dignity that you possess as a child of God and a follower of the Son of God.

January 14, 2010
Jesus

Listening to My voice requires training and discipline. It has often happened that I am goaded. People who do not follow Me generally in their life will sometimes come to a period of pain and they will then, in their anger, say, "Speak, God, if you are there." My friends, I could speak and often do in those moments. The difficulty is that these distanced children do not know how to listen. They have not practiced hearing the voice of God so they are almost deaf to it. I tell you today, there are those who have dedicated their lives to service to Me who are also nearly deaf to My voice. You feel the seriousness of what I am saying and I am glad. This is a cross to many because I cannot direct these individuals into the compassionate service of each moment that I wish for them. They are working, yes, but they are limited by their undisciplined participation in the personal relationship with Me that they require to love as I love and to serve as I would have them serve. The Savior sighs. I am grateful to all who give their life to Me. My gratitude will accompany those who served me throughout their eternity. But I beg each of you to hear Me. Do you recognize the promptings of the Spirit? I will tell you how you will know. Is your heart often moved to pity? Do you find that there are times when you feel impatience and instead offer gentleness? Are you one who conducts others to peace or do you gather round and contribute condemnation when it is being levied against another? Do you talk about Me or about My enemy? Do you look out at a world in pain and see goodness or do you see darkness everywhere? Please, stop your service long enough each day to listen for My whispers from the cross. I am begging you to love each other. Very often I am rejected but I never stop loving. You must be like Me. Love, regardless of how you are repaid. I cannot force anyone to love Me, dear apostles. But I can love them. I want you to do the same. Love God's children in My name and you will be rewarded. Love for Me.

January 18, 2010
Jesus

Heaven supports you, My dear apostle. This loneliness you feel should not alarm you. While you are serving in exile, away from heaven, you feel that you are apart from something that you crave. This is a good feeling because it shows that you are experiencing the longing for heaven that calls you home. I, too, experienced this longing for heaven. It is an aching feeling. It tells you that there is something else that you should have and it is an accurate indication of your state of affairs. What is this thing that you should have that you do not have? It is union with your Savior. You will feel complete when you have this forever, with no risk of losing this union. Do not think that because you are lonely there is something terribly amiss. You are working out your salvation, serving Me where I have placed you, and that it is as it should be. No doubt, if you are trying, you are moving along in holiness steadily. Perhaps you do not see big advances in holiness that come suddenly. Perhaps you see small steady advances that come with sacrifice and suffering. You are not living according to your wishes, but according to My wishes. You see now that there is a difference between what you would like and what I would like. This is excellent, My beloved one. The paths diverge. You have chosen well.

January 19, 2010
Jesus

So much is clear to you, dear apostle. You know that I am calling you. You know that I urge you to more complete abandonment. I ask for trust that is a decision made by you and lived by you. Decide that you will abandon yourself to My work in each day. Decide that you will trust Me to provide you with all that you need. Ask Me what I need from you and do that instead of doing what you would like to do. Sit in silence with Me so that I can calm you and encourage you. Dear apostle, I want you to be focused on Me and on My presence in your work. I want you to look on yesterday as practice and today as the real test. I know that you feel challenged in trust but you are well able to be at peace with Me. You have trusted Me successfully in the past and that is how we know that you can serve in trust today. Only in complete trust will you be able to rise to the challenges that are in your future. If I did not need this from you, I would not ask it of you. I have so much to teach you about holiness and you will learn quickly if you proceed as I am asking. I send abundant graces to you in your work. See that I am sincere in My promise to be with you in everything.

January 20, 2010
Jesus

If I were to direct you to a course that would bring you closer to Me, would you accept it? Would you walk into this course with joy, singing My praise because I had taken your hand and led you quickly into the heavenly mysteries of holiness? Would you be grateful to Me for choosing you amongst many to be one of My closest companions? Would you recognize the great grace that I had given to you by selecting you to proceed with Me down this course that leads so directly to My heart, even if it were to lead you away from your companions? My beloved one, if you are suffering, be assured that I have chosen you to accompany Me as a close companion. Only in suffering is it possible for Me to visit you with certain heavenly graces. These graces are distinguishable from other graces by the impact they leave on a soul. This impact alters permanently the viewpoint of one who has experienced suffering. Some reject My presence in the cross and become bitter. Poor, poor children of God, who do not see God in their cross. You must pray for them and rejoice if you are one who suffers and understands that your Savior is asking you to accompany Him on the walk to Calvary. Could I abandon you with your suffering? Would such a thing be possible when I, Myself have chosen you to be My closest companion? If you experience the cross, My beloved apostle, you will experience Me, but you must desire My companionship as I desire yours.

January 21, 2010
Jesus

My beloved apostles, do not be downhearted because you suffer. Consider that suffering is learning. What do I teach you in suffering? There are so many advantages and revelations possible in suffering that if you are suffering you should say "Truly, I have embarked upon a course of study. I am studying Jesus in the cross." In this way, you will view your time spent carrying the cross as time spent with intensive learning and intensive advance into things holy. One of the things you will struggle with is temptation to reject the cross and rebel against the cross. Anyone who is carrying a cross will experience this because carrying a cross of suffering requires exertion. You must exert yourself to remain faithful and recollected when you are carrying a cross. This is wearisome at times. But the fact that one is tired does not mean that one is finished. If the cross has not diminished then you must carry it for a time longer. I am the personal instructor of those carrying crosses. Do you listen carefully to your instructor? Do you seek to remain close to Me? If you do, I will teach you how to carry the cross in the way that benefits you most, and by benefitting you, remember that heaven benefits all around you and all that is close to your heart. Just as the Father blessed many through My Passion, He will bless many through yours. You are not alone. I am with you.

January 22, 2010
Jesus

Your anguish is particular to you as My anguish was particular to Me. Only God knew the full extent of My suffering in the Passion. Between the Father and the Son, the Spirit flowed with complete knowledge of every aspect of My sorrow. My dear apostle, you are suffering in ways that nobody understands. I know this. I know that you have private wounds and I know these wounds as if they were My own. All of your suffering is open to My gaze, which means that I am the only one who can console you effectively. Because others do not grasp the full extent of your pain or the reasons for it, others cannot provide the exact remedies. Only I, Jesus Christ, can do that. Others can be compassionate company for you and I hope that you are compassionate company for others but for true comfort that enables you to continue on in service with courage and patient endurance, you will need Me. You will need your Savior, just as your Savior needs you. We are in a situation of mutual need. My heart craves your safety and happiness. You crave My love and soothing presence. Come more and more deeply into My heart and you will find that holiness is yours. It will become a surprise to you when you see how far you have come because you will not be concentrating on yourself and your movement away from self but on Me and on movement deeper into heaven's plan. Do you see? When you are working for My goals in your day, you do not notice the spiritual gains you are making. You do not really feel the growth because I am the artist of your soul who is creating a beautiful image of the divine in you. You are the willing canvas who allows the Savior to work. Do not rebel against My plan for you. Rejoice in My desire for union with you. Decide today to move more completely into My plan for your holiness.

The Vertical Relationship

A man can best bring about God's Kingdom on earth if he is connected to Jesus Christ in a vertical relationship. Only then will the man, created by God to serve God's interests, be alert to the heavenly goal in each moment. All that is good proceeds from this one truth, that God and man remain together in the Spirit.

God is the source of all goodness. We know Jesus with the Spirit and strive to remain in that Spirit through love that bonds the Savior and the saved. The Spirit is love, the love which unites. Some make simple statements such as "God is love," and I believe statements such as this to be true. And yet, there is also a true distinction which distinguishes the Persons of the Father and the Son and the Spirit. Contemplation on these three Persons leads one to a great respect for the vastness of the Invisible Reality. Surely the Father's mercy became most perfectly manifest in the presence of the Son who was delivered to us through an action of the Spirit. If the Person of Jesus Christ is the best model for mankind, then it is through unity with Him that we will become our most perfect selves, and fulfill God's greatest goals for our time on earth. When we look back on our lives with the full understanding of perfect truth, we will look hungrily for the times when we best modelled Christ.

Oh dear, this is a very big undertaking, to persuade others that their best hope, their biggest mandate, is to embark with total commitment on a journey that is the most important journey that they will ever take and that is the one that proceeds directly into a vertical relationship with Jesus Christ.

We must define vertical. Webster's dictionary states that "vertical suggests a line or direction rising straight upward toward a zenith." This provides a good visual image. Our eyes should be always raised upwards. The whole story of the coming of God's kingdom is the relationship between each one of us and Jesus Christ. The success of our vocation depends largely on how well we participate in the relationship with Jesus Christ because in order to serve the King, we must possess the King. To possess the King, we must allow the King to possess us. We must welcome

Jesus into our soul and then let our lives become more and more perfectly ordered to His will. It is about the man and Jesus, Jesus and the man, united in service through the Spirit to the Father. If Jesus has someone who is willing to remain in a vertical relationship with Him, He can then flow out horizontally to others more or less directly from heaven through the Spirit. This is so beautiful, so sublime. What we then offer to others is heavenly and heavenly-ordered, resplendent with healing and affirming graces. Others can absorb from us what is good and life-giving, even though we remain imperfect in our humanity because we can become more and more adept at serving others from Christ, as opposed to serving others from our imperfect self.

To understand this best, we can rest in the glimpses of heaven that we have received through this apostolate. It is true that we partially understand heaven to be union with Christ. The saints interact with joy because all is Christ-centered interaction, devoid of selfish motive. The greater the strength of the vertical relationship with Jesus on earth, the more we can interact like the saints in heaven interact, that is, serving together on a parallel course with the horizontal connection strengthening each one's vertical relationship to Christ. There can be human cravings to abandon God's goals for selfish goals but if we do this we will not strengthen either the individual relationship to Jesus Christ or the human relationship between two people. Actions outside of the Spirit cannot strengthen us because such actions take us out of the divine will for each person. Many, many human relationships are this way and while they do not bring about the coming of God's kingdom, they can, at times, result in God's love when there is sacrifice, one for another.

January 11, 2010

The Lord asks us to serve Him. He calls us into service and we answer the call and begin to do His work. But it is true that many begin to do His work and forget that the biggest part of the work is to become transformed. This need to be transformed is ongoing, daily, and sometimes even hourly. It must be viewed as such because if we do not view it as such we will be doing God's work according to our human inspirations. Dear apostles, how many have encountered religious people only to be hurt terribly and disappointed terribly by their arguably unreligious behaviors and actions. We have all experienced this. Being hurt by someone is one thing but being hurt by someone who claims to serve God is another thing entirely. There is huge temptation to bitterness and huge temptation to justify a rejection of God Himself, or His Church, based on what some people do in His name.

Some people work in the world and then are prompted to serve the Church for example. They take their places on parish councils and church committees and then they claw and scramble for power and control. They want to be the best and the most important. Does Jesus need their help? Of course. Do we need their fellowship as Christians? Undoubtedly. But there must be an understanding that to serve Jesus effectively we must serve as Jesus would serve.

Also, I fear that if the laity is to take her place in the Church as leaders, their whole spirit will need to be purified. The laity, according to Vatican II, are uniquely placed in the world and can witness where God has placed us. We are called to bring Gospel teachings and principles to others wherever we find ourselves. That is the first part and every situation we encounter will have a heavenly response and a heavenly action available to us. These responses and actions will be known to us through the Spirit Whom we will only come to know in prayer.

The second part is our call to serve alongside priests, bishops and cardinals as leaders in the Church, helping to bring about the forward momentum of the Church being revealed by God. But, dear lay apostles, we must be worthy of this call. We must be reverent about what Jesus is asking from us. We have a role to play, yes, but we will not fill the role unless we serve as victims to the role. A priest walks in the footsteps of the First Victim. We must also walk in those footsteps. 'All for the glory of God,' must be our constant refrain. We must expect to offer pride and admiration and even human respect in exchange for God's will being done through us and around us. At times this can be shockingly hurtful and painful. Let us note in advance that it will not be fair so that we have no expectation of being treated fairly. John the Baptist proclaimed the coming of Jesus Christ and as a reward he was arrested and then martyred. Many who made a path for Christ were treated in the same way. Are we willing to offer service, in humility and love, and in exchange be treated as Jesus and the saints were treated? That is the call, dear friends. That is the call.

I believe we are willing and I believe we will be found worthy. But we need to know how.

To start, we must come into every single service as a servant, there to serve others and help them to best do their jobs. Leadership is not something a holy person will grab for, never mind wrestle away from someone else without a mandate. Leaders should be loved and supported and respected as representatives of God in the Church. I have said this before but it bears repeating if a Church leader is getting it wrong, pray for him or her. Help him or her in any way possible but do not be one who spreads scandal and criticism.

January 11, 2010

It is possible that some lay people who serve the Church have a relationship with the Church that is developed and a relationship with Jesus Christ that is undeveloped. The only way to do justice to our commitment to the Church is to make a greater commitment to our relationship with Jesus Christ. This can be difficult to maintain because, like the mother in the busy household, the work can take over.

I remember a mother explaining that she became so obsessed with matching socks that she implemented strict rules about clothing and the placement of clothing. It became ridiculous and in a moment of illumination she realized that she had completely missed the point of mothering, focusing instead on regimenting the household and the children to a degree that was counterproductive and actually hurtful. With the illumination came the ability to laugh at the obsessive nature of her campaign.

To look further into this, it is clear that the mother's over-reaction was based on a feeling of being overwhelmed. She had one standard of housecleaning before the children came and afterwards had difficulty making the adjustment to heading a children's home rather than an adult's home. The over-reaction was understandable as she feared she was failing when she failed to maintain a higher level of organization. Perhaps the reader feels I have lost my track but I am trying to say that when this woman became a mother, her priorities had to shift in order to remain in the divine will. To remain with Christ in her day, she had to enter into the loving and nurturing of her young children more than in the structure of material possessions. It had to be about the children and not the protection of material things.

Many priests, too, find themselves with administrative tasks that can feel overwhelming and which can frustrate their fathering instincts. Possibly, a priest must be allowing Christ to transmit the graces of the sacraments through him to feel fulfilled and remain in touch with his vocation. Clearly, some priests are necessary for administrative work that is vital to the Church but each should have an area of his life where he remains connected to his priestly ministry. Lay people chosen to work alongside priests must be alert to relieving some of the burden of non-priestly duties in order to free the priest for priestly duties.

The fulfillment of Vatican II, where the laity comes more directly into the stream of service in the Church, will be fraught with difficulties. Humanity being what it is, the transition will not be smooth. But it has been heralded as the future of the Church and as such we must all do our part to move the Church closer to its realization.

Imagine a Church filled with those possessing the spirit of the servant. It will be so beautiful.

January 12, 2010

It can be dangerous to be around someone who is pretending to have good will toward others. The truth comes out, of course, but it is for this reason that many are put-off by Christianity or, indeed, any religion. Who can blame them? One who is searching will look at distortions in faith and simply continue searching. He will not say, "Ah, I have found that which I seek in this group where I find those who pretend to be good but really are not." People are sensitive to truth when they are searching. It is for this reason that we need to work continually on transforming ourselves because if we pause at all, we will continue to talk the talk out of habit but be at risk of not walking the walk. I am becoming trite. Let me say it another way.

We have all been fooled. There are those who mimic holiness and I have no doubt that they do great good and that they perhaps actually desire to do good. What is wrong? They are really seeking self-glorification. They, at some point, must have seen and craved the admiration given to someone who was holy. They, craving this admiration for themselves, began to mimic the one who is holy. This is basically how we all do it, for the record, in that we model ourselves on someone whom we believe to possess the traits we desire. But here is the difference. One is real and the other is false. When one sees the real one, one can readily identify the fake because it is like comparing an orange to a picture of an orange. The real orange will be nourishing and the picture of the orange will be ornamental. One gets tired of looking at a picture of an orange when one is hungry and thirsty. One is grateful for the nourishment which comes from the real orange.

Now a picture is not hard to distinguish from the real thing if you have eyes that can see. Even then, there are times when the image is so good that you have to stare at it for some time before you can see it is a fake.

In the holiness life, those who mimic can be masterful. They can learn the language, adapt the mannerisms and absorb, to the most astounding degree, the habits of holy people they have known. This makes them good imposters. They come with a proclaimed desire to serve and can appear very holy and adaptable but eventually there will be trouble because these imposters have problems with jealousy and envy and they will turn on someone who possesses true holiness and target them. They will rebel against any direct authority, ingratiating them to the larger authority or ingratiating them to the lesser authority and sowing dissension against the higher authority. There is always some type of teaming and the goal always seems to be divisiveness. These people are often attention-seeking and their claim will be one of victimization. "I am a victim," will be their constant refrain. And yet honey drips from their words and a pretense of compassion abounds. They want to be treated with deference. They want to be viewed as important and superior. This can be quite shocking in its extent when one does not expect it and one is inclined to disbelieve the truth of this matter because the truth is so dreadfully revolting. One is inclined to say, "Surely, I am wrong about what I observe." Often, one must be convinced but when one has seen it a few times, one needs less convincing and one is inclined to be swift in identifying such individuals and limiting one's interactions.

How do we separate ourselves from those who are destructive? We all have similar temptations, if the truth be told. We may crave attention, want to be admired and have rebellious thoughts against authority. So it is good to see that often our claim of holiness is not one we can back up in every moment. But here is the difference between your average struggling apostle and the one who is a fake. The average struggling apostle (most of us fall into this category) knows he is no saint. He has a realistic attitude about his gaps in holiness and he is striving to do better. He understands that to protect God's interests, he has to exert himself and even then God's interests are at risk from his humanity. The average struggling apostle will have the ability to laugh at himself when he is ridiculous and he will have a good working knowledge of his weaknesses and temptations.

These others are not in touch with either their capacity for good or their instinct for destruction. They destruct at will. Wherever they go there is tearing down, drama, condemnation of others and judgment. Superiority comes out in regular waves like the rings emitted from a tracking device. They move, the superiority shifts to others but it keeps coming off them. Regardless of how much praising of God they do with their lips, eventually anger shows up because there is not enough attention in the world for them. Perhaps those reading this will wonder if in writing about this I am passing judgment. Be assured, I am convinced there are mitigating circumstances which will result in merciful treatment of those who behave this way. My goal in illuminating these things is to warn apostles to be alert to false representatives of holiness. They are a danger to our peace and to God's work. They infiltrate our organizations and groups and create all manner of upheaval.

How often we witness a holy apostle being compassionate and accepting ill-treatment in these situations, consistently returning love for hostility and overlooking attacks. It is good to try to achieve a good outcome and give others every possible benefit of the doubt but, at some point, one must tell a holy apostle, "This person holds ill will for you. You cannot fix this person." There are times when we have to move decisively to protect ourselves or our work from such imposters. One prays for them and hopes they fare well but one also sees, with experience, that these situations tend to follow these people. Wherever they go there are flashes of upheaval and distress, disunity and division. This is good to see as it confirms the right judgment but bad to see as others are suffering. This is the reality though, so, we look at it and protect ourselves through vigilant prayer.

January 14, 2010

Yes, it is true. A man can best bring about God's Kingdom on earth if He is connected to Jesus Christ in a vertical relationship. Our heaven will be spent in union with Jesus Christ. Our earth, this time of service, must also be spent in this way. Poor Jesus has so much to tell us, so much counsel to whisper into our hearts. We look at a person and perhaps we see the obvious failure, perhaps in an addiction or a broken marriage or in destitution or poverty or in criminal behavior or sinfulness. Jesus, just then when our glance falls upon them, whispers His goal, how He wishes to love them, console them or minister to them physically. He needs us to speak of mercy, yes, but mercy that comes from His heart, united to our heart. This will be the mercy that packs power to change and carries heavy graces that result in miraculous comfort and conversion. The difference in being connected to Christ and not being connected to Christ is this. The mercy coming from someone who is not connected comes from a place of self, humanity that is always looking for something selfish, some return on their investment of assistance or love. If we have a vertical relationship with Jesus Christ, we offer Him, not us. There is purity and abandonment. We seek nothing and we expect and often experience derision and ingratitude so we are not stunned or disappointed at such a return for our investment. We are investing Christ, not ourselves. When we are attacked, we offer Jesus, absorbing the attack in our bodies and hearts as Jesus absorbed His Passion in His body and heart. But the attacks do not cripple us or paralyze us. We learn to not count these attacks as personal.

It is apparent that those who lack the vertical relationship will feel wounds very painfully and they will object to ill treatment. None of us like to be put out, slandered, insulted or otherwise mistreated in our humanity, if truth be told. But we know it is part of our service and part of our following in the footsteps of the First Victim. But it is clear that those who lack this vertical relationship will fold very quickly when there is suffering and hardship. Real offering is not attractive. There will very quickly be rebellion, pinned onto something else. Oh dear, these who serve from a place of self as opposed to a place of unity are not very hardy at all. These are the ones who end up cynical and superior. Isn't that a contradiction? And yet, there it is. This is why the saints fled from notice and honors. These things are embarrassing when held up against real self-abandonment.

We must make a commitment to contemplative prayer. It is only in contemplative prayer, sitting often at the foot of the crucifix, that we can truly absorb the nature of the One we follow. We move deeper and deeper into unity, into this relationship and then Jesus Himself flows out from us horizontally into the relationships we have with others. We advance together up the mountain of holiness and can only in this model of service pull each other up. We can advance as a group if we are connected to Christ. If there is not enough vertical about the individuals in our organizations or families, and it becomes too much about the horizontal, we will see systemic failure in our families, religious organizations and faith communities.

Vertical first, then horizontal.

Let all of our faith community be about the vertical first, then the horizontal. We must advance further into discipline in this regard and then we will offer a truly counter-cultural statement.

January 17, 2010

It can happen that a follower of God hears a call to service. It is an accurate call. He chooses well and answers with a yes answer that draws the follower into God's work. But, if there is no proper formation and guidance, that follower can embark upon this lifetime of service with no real relationship with Jesus Christ. I think this might happen more than we know. That is not a good thought, or a restful thought, but I think it might be true. What do we have then? A good person, committed to Christ, who does not know Him and who is destined to fall into disappointment and possibly cynicism. It is not enough to talk about holy concepts. One has to live holy concepts. Some of the people who speak with the most knowledge are absolutely lost when it comes to living these concepts and that is because they lack an honest and vertical relationship with Jesus Christ. This is not a statement of judgment, but warning. We must first be alert ourselves to the symptoms that our vertical relationship is disconnected. We must be alert in a daily way. And next we must be alert to the symptoms of this in others with whom we serve or for whom we are charged with supervision. Sometimes a person can be doing a very good job but be dreadfully sad on the inside. A priest once confided, "I really don't know what I'm doing here." This was a perfectly natural need for renewal, of course and this priest was serving seamlessly for years, but he had become temporarily disconnected from his relationship with Jesus.

The service of a wife must be ordered to her husband through Jesus. If the wife gets too busy about the work, she can forget about why she is doing it. She is part of a sacramental union for which she will be called to give an account. How sad will it be if, upon her death, she offers Jesus a house that was orderly and a husband who was unloved?

We must each consider this very seriously. Whatever the vocation, it cannot be about the work first. It must be first about the *why* of the work. Why are we doing this work? Who called us into it? Whose work is it, after all? Is it our work? We can only offer limited humanity which is self-serving. Or is it God's work? If so, we had better remain in the closest possible contact with God so that we are offering God in the work.

The vertical relationship ensures that Jesus Christ flows through us and insures that we remain on course, never losing the way. Jesus, during His time on earth, was really with the people in front of Him. A vertical relationship with Jesus will insure that we are also truly with the people in front of us in a loving way.

January 19, 2010

If we are connected to Jesus in a vertical relationship, we will model trust. This is such a powerful example to others. Often, through our trust, we can help to allay the fears of those around us. This is what humanity does best for each other. When we encounter a person trusting Jesus Christ, often our fear is diminished. Everyone has, at times, seen an example of trust in the Lord that stands out. When this occurs, we are left considering how to practice similar trust. If God's kingdom is to come, we will all have to live out trust so that we can help those around us to serve calmly and peacefully, resting always in the providence of heaven. Apostles should be models of trust. We should live trust in such a way that others look to us and find reassurance. This is God's plan. Clearly, dear friends, if we will not live our trust and show humanity how to trust, who will do so?

We are chosen to be receptacles of Christ's love during this period of transition. We are chosen to be a well where others can come to drink of God's love. Sometimes, all that is necessary for this to happen is that we not judge another. The absence of judgment, all by itself, is a happening worthy of remark. In this time, judgment flows out readily, in an unchecked way. Rivers of judgment and condemnation stream past humanity in foul waterways that crisscross our days. Judging is a pastime and pronouncing condemnation is a sport. Self-examination, something that *is* our business, is not nearly as common place. This is sad because those who look only outward will not find Christ, Who rests within. Self-examination is the activity that should be consuming us.

Admissions of mistakes are imperative for each of us, that is, unless we never make mistakes. In the same way, false admissions and false self-examination is as distasteful as everything false and is as putrid as all deceit. There is nothing more off-putting than one who claims to be self-examining when in fact he is simply putting on a show of self-examining. It is not good to witness someone who lays a claim to small mistakes to distract from sinister emotions and large acts of malice. Such falseness is an attempt to hold up a mask of humility which conceals writhing and angry pride. The word haughty comes to my mind. With this we will always see rage. The one who tries to tear the mask aside will face an outpouring of hatred that is chilling but God protects.

January 26, 2010

Yes, we are involved in circles of service with others and those who will bring the most from their circles are those who possess a vertical commitment to Jesus Christ. It is for that reason that it is in the best interest of heaven, and the Returning King we serve, to lift others up to their vertical relationship with Jesus. We can be patient and kind, loving and tolerant, all the while returning love for hostility and setting an example and praying that the other will heed God's promptings for the service destined to be performed in the circle. If, as happens, there are times when another will not accept the example, the love and the grace-prompted duties of the circle with us, then perhaps the circle evaporates and we part company from someone. This is not to be confused with the sacramental union of marriage, although that is of course a circle of service but marriage carries the vocational commitment that other relationships do not. I believe there are many lost opportunities in life, many instances when one or the other refuses to serve as Jesus wants him to serve and the result is a circle of hope dissolved. I say circle of hope because each circle of service carries with it heavenly hope. Heaven connects two people, sending grace for the goals. The reason the lay apostolate is so important is because Jesus is sending unique graces for this period of mankind's spiritual history and this period of the development of His bride, the Church. He hopes that each apostle will allow heaven to flow through him with graces of clarity which will direct him to the heavenly goal in each circle of service. What heaven can then achieve is exponentially advanced in terms of effective outcome. I believe we will see shorter and more abrupt conversions with deeper commitments, calling more people into the religious life and priesthood, and, equally, if not more importantly, in terms of perfecting the model of Church, a laity who are truly co-responsible, as committed to the coming of God's kingdom as the clergy and religious. These groups, working alongside each other, will be cells of holiness and purity of intention ready to be instantly 'deployed' for a heavenly purpose.

People working in cells of holiness can protect each other better than people working on holiness alone. What one cannot see jumps out at another. Perhaps we will see groups of people, cells or even prayer groups, advancing up the mountain of holiness together, tethered as it were, for safety. God is so good to not only send these graces, but to name them for us so that we can make the most possible use of them.

Divine Mercy

It is clear that as each ray of mercy comes from the heart of Jesus, it finds its intended target and surrounds it, meaning, of course, each person. This ray of mercy which surrounds each person waits until the person is ready or perhaps willing. It is true that some people never allow themselves to be closed off from mercy. They remain connected to their baptismal grace throughout their lives. It is also true that some, through sin, turn their faces away from mercy and try to go it alone. Life is lonely for them in a different way than the loneliness of the follower.

When one has turned one's face away from mercy, that is, the individual ray of mercy intended for one which is the Vertical Relationship, that person becomes alone, regardless of the people he may surround himself with. Conversely, a person could be completely isolated from other people and never be alone because his face is turned into the ray of mercy that propels itself out from the Father, through the Savior by the power of the Spirit. Lonely and alone are two very different things. When one has rejected God's mercy, there is the decision to be without God, and one's loneliness brings one to bitterness. When one accepts God's mercy and one is alone, that loneliness brings one to a longing for heaven and a pity and compassion for the plight of others who do not understand what they crave, that is, God.

Now the man surrounded by darkness, by choice, has only to turn his face into the ray of mercy that exists for him but the brightness sometimes makes him afraid. It hurts his eyes, so to speak. What does the Savior do? He sends in a candle, carried by an apostle. This candle is the smallest example of mercy, of course, but it is a measure that the person in darkness can examine without being blinded and overcome. Small doses, often, so to speak. This candlelight is a crumb from the loaf and the starving man often examines it before allowing enough hope to actually ingest it. The starving man thinks, 'Can it truly be for me? Is it a mirage, a cruel hoax, that if I lift this crumb of bread to my lips I will not be pounced upon by wild dogs for which it is really intended?'

Dearest reader, do not underestimate the effects of starvation on those who have rejected God's light and have lived for a time in darkness. It can be extremely difficult to convince them that not only does God desire them in His presence, God requires them in His presence for His kingdom to come. In my meanderings on drawing God's children back to His heart, I often think that we must draw them back through need. They will be more likely to come as assistants than as recipients. "Please, help us," is a more palatable and earnest invitation than "Come, pitiful wretch." Often, the greatest act of kindness one can offer is to be needy and vulnerable. Dearest apostles, take this to your hearts and let your pride dissipate into the air. It is nearly foolproof to allow a person to experience his own goodness as a means to draw him into greatness. Often, when a child experiences his innate goodness, he, in wonder and tremulous hope, advances quite quickly into virtue.

We are all children.

I intended to concentrate on the effect of God's mercy because I believe that this effect is the story of this time, however, I advanced a step out ahead of myself into the transformative goal, that is, the spread of the Good News. Because I am out on that rock in this pond of consideration, I will work from there for the moment.

We are transformed when we turn our faces into the ray of mercy that is intended for us and we then, as a reflexive action, begin to decipher how it is that God wants to use our presence. We have to share the mercy. There is no other meaningful way to continue our earthly existence. The mercy will not stay in us. It grows and swells in order to move through us. When an opportunity for sharing this mercy presents itself, the mercy explodes from us in a gush of grace. This can happen in a chance encounter with a stranger, it always calls itself forth for those closest to us of course, but it also occurs as an ongoing stream in our ministries or chosen professions. Once God establishes Himself in a soul, He makes His presence count. The soul, working with and from God, will do anything to protect the stream. It accepts all manner of suffering and sacrifice, struggling in sadness on the days when the acceptance is grudging. What a cross this becomes for the apostle.

The apostle longs for a joyful acceptance of the suffering and sacrifice because the apostle knows this is possible and yet it seems to be denied to the apostle. "Where is my joy?" can be the lament of the willing apostle. How can God stand to work through one who constantly bemoans the need to reject self-will? Truly, that is the mystery of the Incarnation. God is willing to work not only with us, but through us. God is willing to humble Himself and pin His Renewal, so to speak, on the trembling nature of our offerings. It makes one ask, "What is a saint?"

I believe that a saint must simply be that person who is willing to work surrounded and reproached constantly by his imperfection.

May 25, 2010

Yes, our imperfection surrounds us. Our lack of holiness reproaches us. Where do we get the courage to continue on in the service to the Lord? We get the courage from that ray of mercy which proceeds out to us. This courage is radical in the sense that the study of the Lord puts us not closer to Him in terms of His perfection but further away in terms of understanding the reality of our condition. The closer we get to Jesus, the more we realize the distance between our condition and His perfection. We receive this light about our condition but at the same time, in the same increments, the Lord sends enhanced knowledge of His mercy. If these two things were not revealed more or less concurrently or in similar increments, we could not stand it. Often one jogs ahead of the other, which creates mystical storms. But without courage we would be unable to continue on in close service to heaven given our pitiful state of 'lacking'. We understand that we lack purity of intention, abandonment, and trust. Oh dear, where would we stop the discussion of those things we lack? We might never stop. Better to talk about what we have and that is the constant grace of heaven. We have a limitless stream of mercy, for ourselves and for anyone else we wish to offer it to. If we can acknowledge briefly what we lack each day, just for a moment or two, and then bathe in what we have, infinite Divine Mercy, we will have the courage and boldness we require.

A man in the hospital lay quite still. All was still except his eyes. His eyes watched everything and everyone. When a conversation began, he disclosed that he was paralyzed from the waist down. He immediately began to talk about all that he *had*, the movement of his hands, his intellect, etc. Someone remarked that he spoke very positively given his condition. He wondered aloud how he could *not* be positive given the intercession of Our Lady of Fatima.

This man was not only a recipient of God's mercy, he was a source of God's mercy because the minute he spoke, he talked about God's mercy which enabled it to flow out to those who listened. This man's experience of God's mercy, via the intercession of Our Lady, placed in him a supply of mercy so great that his reflexive action was to share it. He could not contain it or hoard it.

This is the opposite of worldly reflex which would encourage us to hoard treasure. That is how we distinguish heavenly treasure from earthly treasure. With earthly treasure, we keep it, store it, save it and give from it sparingly. There is pain in losing it and being separated from it. With heavenly treasure, we give it freely if we have it and we feel only joy in sharing it. What we possess, in terms of heavenly treasure, we offer to others with rejoicing, praying that others will recognize its value. Words cannot do justice to the value of what we bring to those in darkness. Only the Spirit within us, studying closely what we have received, can communicate the extent of what God wishes to send through us to others. To become the recipient of heaven's grace is a great thing. To become a source of heaven's grace for others, let us call this a heavenly outpost on earth, is an even greater thing.

Ten lepers were healed. One returned to offer gratitude. The others no doubt experienced thanksgiving and gratitude but did not offer thanksgiving to the Source. Which leper shall we emulate, dear friends?

In this apostolate, we must emulate the one who returned to give thanks. We do this by assuming our share of the burden of this Renewal, in whatever capacity God requires, in total humility.

While we are on earth, we will not do things our way, but God's way. There will be sacrifice. We will sacrifice self-will. When we get to heaven, in return, God will let us do things our way in the sense that our intercessory desires for those on earth will become God's as well. He will give this to us in advance, also, of course, in that His gratitude to us for our service will be shown by His advancing our 'interests' even during our time of service here. If we pray for someone, the Lord, who is always like the leper who returned, meaning He is always grateful for our fidelity and any acts of kindness to His cause, will bless those around us.

One life, one commitment given in totality has the most enormous ramifications. The amount of consolation God can bring through one life to other lives is infinite given the ripple effect of love. Who will give in totality? Who will abandon himself completely? Will it be you? Me? Is He asking someone else or is He asking us? I think, dear apostles, He is asking us. I think heaven hopes we will answer "Yes," without condition.

Is it embarrassing that we give our service with stipulations? Perhaps that is the best we can do on a given day, that is, serve to some degree. Perhaps though, if we remain firmly anchored in the present, we can give everything. And perhaps, if we become accustomed to abandonment in the present, God can teach us to accept joy.

May 26, 2010

Heaven seeks, on each day, to illuminate for us more fully the Invisible Reality. Those who have eyes will see, of course, and will advance in holiness given the correct disposition. And this disposition is that of the slave. Such a flash word! Slave? The word evokes the most negative images in human history. The slave is allowed no self-interest, no self-will, and no self-determination. What kind of life is this for any man?

This is the constant call of heaven, that is, to separate earthly thinking from heavenly thinking. Those who have experienced

God's mercy and who turn their faces into it, bathe in it as it were, will throw themselves at the foot of the Throne and say, "God, I am so unworthy but I am willing and eager to serve you. Not to lead you, God, but to serve you." In our lifetime as an apostle, we will do this again and again because in our lifetime as an apostle, we will forget why we serve, again and again. We have only to re-experience our weakness and we are brought back to the foot of the Throne with gratitude that Jesus allows us to serve at all.

Dear apostles, how calmly I consider our collective inadequacy. It is a poor apostle indeed who sees no need for another drink from the fountain of Mercy. If we identify our gaps, we will seek to fill them from God. If we do not identify our gaps, we will be like the bugle that sounds no call or the silent harp. We will blunder through our lives, making ourselves an emotional burden on others with our self-interest and pomposity. This has been stated before and bears re-stating. If one cannot think of any areas where improvement is needed, one should ask those closest to one. The wise apostle should throw himself on the mercy of those who know him, presuming some level of good will in those around him, and ask for illumination. This act of humility will benefit both in some way and God will determine the benefit.

It is true that one has great difficulty identifying progress in the holiness walk. Climbing the mountain seems tedious because it involves step after step after step. Many apostles will say, "Dear me, I am still at this for so many years and I am no holier." This is possible but not probable. If one has been walking, one has most likely been strengthening muscles. More likely, it is the case that the incline has grown steeper and the apostle is still walking, the operative word being *still*. If we keep walking, we are in the holiness game. We have not abandoned the mountain for the valley. We realize we have not reached the summit and we understand the relationship between nourishment, meaning prayer, and stamina, meaning continued service in God's work.

It is evident that a person who is caressed by God's mercy in a daily way will resemble a child who is completely secure. The child is a breathing, living testament to the mercy of God. It can be seen in the eyes. In the eyes there is no agenda other than to love. In the eyes there is no furtiveness, no slyness. There is openness to both give and receive love.

We really must show up and stay, as has been stated. Not everyone looks exactly the same so we must look at others and consider that even while they do not look exactly like us, perhaps this is how they look when they are staying. This is their way of staying. There can be great crosses on the mountain and the crosses form us and change us and often we do not look our best when God is forming us and changing us. We will experience pain during this process. A look of pain and suffering in the eyes of a brother or sister does not mean, necessarily, that they are disconnected from Divine Mercy. Perhaps it is only Divine Mercy that sustains them, that keeps them staggering forward on this mountain. What am I saying? I am not sure except that we must concern ourselves with our own disposition and focus on how purely we can love in each moment.

If an apostle wanted a model, in addition to Jesus, Mary and the saints, I would suggest that this apostle look for someone who possesses humility. We must cast our eyes around and find someone who is truly humble. We must emulate that person. This will always be a person who is willing to listen. This will be a person who has suffered. This will be someone who has been in service for some period of time. Anyone can be humble for a week, but for an extended period? Under duress and insult? This is the person to be our model. This person will be willing to be corrected, to be wrong. This person will accept counsel and be teachable, regardless of his position in either the world or the Church. The mind and heart will be open to joy and rejoicing.

We must avoid intellectual seduction at all costs, dear apostles. Be impressed by holiness, not intellectualism. If someone holds himself above us because of his education, this is only evidence that he has self-examination left undone. Perhaps this person does not understand the need to learn constantly. We must pray we avoid this mistake ourselves.

When we get to heaven we will see the exact nature of our limited knowledge, wherever we are at in the learning scale of the world. We will be dazzled by our ignorance, radiant in our lack of wisdom. All of heaven will resound with the hymn of our kindergarten level of knowing.

If we are to be experts in anything, dear apostles, let us be experts in humility and experts in the awareness of the limitations of our understanding of God's kingdom which is simply love.

As an apostolate, Jesus has charged us with the instruction of promoting unity in the Church. Remember that for unity to occur, everyone must move into greater charity. Do not be tricked into thinking that for unity to occur, everyone else must move so they can stand where we are standing. Let us be honest, dear apostles. Let us admit that at some time we thought we had all the answers, that when everyone finally agreed with us, God's kingdom would come.

Do not rebel against this truth because God, in His perfect wisdom, sees that it is so. A deep breath is necessary here for all of us, regardless of our place in the kingdom, of our beliefs, our youthful arrogance and mistakes.

Let us consider that wherever we are today, whatever our beliefs, we have just been reprimanded. God wants us to do better, not tomorrow, but today and every day. For unity to be achieved, everyone must move. For many apostles, I think most, this will mean simply learning how to better love those who hold different positions.

May 27, 2010

It is true that many feel isolated, even in religious life. Many have said, "Oh dear. I am so alone. My fellow religious or fellow priests do not understand the movement of the Spirit in these times.

They are closed off to the Spirit and this leaves me feeling isolated and alone."

Dear apostles, I have many things to say about this.

First, Christ felt alone in the Garden. Period. If we feel alone, let us rejoice in the fact that we are able to share His pain. Also, for the permanent record, we are all lonely, in one way or another.

Secondly, the experience of not fitting in or not being understood by our fellow servants in no way diminishes our mandate to love them, to travel miles in order to be next to them in the place where they are standing. If we do not agree with them about theology, private revelation or the current condition or movement of the Church, perhaps we should avoid those conversations initially and talk about cars, gardening or whatever else is of interest to them.

It is a divine mandate that we love. It is not a divine mandate that we agree in all things. There is a tendency to 'hang around' with only those who are on our exact page. This is counterproductive to unity and will, believe me, please, result in ugly teaming and superiority. Better we reach out in love and establish relationships where we should.

"But they do not like me," the apostle protests. We are not saying to establish best-friend relationships, but periodic interactions where the apostle loves unconditionally will move us all toward unity. Yes, we will put up with something to make this happen. We will accept jibes, perhaps, maybe teasing, ridiculing and we will answer with love. Dear apostles, I knew an apostle who once decided to love unconditionally to such a degree that he was certain the recipient thought him an imbecile. There was no let up in his love, however, and eventually this resulted in capitulation and a mutually loving relationship with a person who formerly had nothing but antipathy toward him. God's kingdom came in this situation and it came through love!

Love, and the decision to love, resulted in a willingness to absorb being misunderstood for a long period of time. The payoff at the end was sublime and the incidents of hurt along the way were considered beneficial for the person himself and so he offered them willingly for the target of his love campaign.

Dear apostles, many priests feel that they are triangles in square holes in terms of fellowship with fellow priests. Clearly, the priest himself is content where he is but perhaps he looks different to the other priests or he is younger or of a different strain of spirituality or what have you. Let me talk about the serious temptation that comes with this. It can come over time so try to be alert to the initial rumblings.

Dearest fathers of God's children, you must reach out to other priests, in love. To use loose terms, maybe one is traditional and one is progressive, both within the proper boundaries of Church truth and life. Both feel they have it right and perhaps both are accurately representing God's unique presence in his priesthood. All is well except for one thing. Neither allows for the possibility that the other is serving authentically according to God's plan for him in his priesthood. Neither allows for the possibility that the other is on the correct path marked out for him. Both have niggling temptations to dislike each other and superiority that he may or may not even identify, never mind combat. Because of the polarized positions, neither recognizes or accepts his obligation to actively support and love the other.

From the outside, it is clear that we need many representations of Christ if we are going to effectively minister to many different types of people. Individuality is essential in God's kingdom. Will we accept individuality in an orchestra but not in humanity? Heaven is not about rigid conformance but spectacular transformation. Our uniqueness is unarguable so how can we become smug that others do not live out their vocations as we live out ours.

This phenomenon is clear also with parenting. Young parents struggle to shape the family's identity. As they do, they look at other families and often say, "We are not like that." This is fair enough and "Well done" to them for searching out their unique selves. The problem is when they draw the conclusion that, "because we are not like them, we are better." This is a bad tone to inject in any family identity because it is the opposite of the truth. Better to say, "We live this way. Not everyone does. The fact that not everyone lives like us does not mean we should change and it does not mean they should change."

We cannot force another family or another person to change. We also know that even if we are serving now, it is possible that we were not always serving as well. And if we are serving well today, there is a risk, always, that we will not serve as well tomorrow. And when that happens, are we as prepared to proclaim our mistakes as loudly as we proclaimed our superiority? I have not seen this in myself, dear friends, or others. So it is best that we relax into our identity and at the same time, assume that God's plan can look different in the identity of those around us.

If we accept God's mercy each day, He will show us those around us in merciful light. We will view them in God's mercy and this mercy will soften and often eradicate the judgments emerging from our frail humanity and limited understanding. Jesus views everyone with love. This love is gentle.

For a beneficial experiment, we must make a decision to move into a day and study those around us, perhaps especially those with whom we often disagree, and view them in God's total mercy. We can safely promise that this experience will change our viewpoint. May Jesus help us to accept our past failures but imagine if we began every single day determined to engage in this experiment.

We would have both a unified Church and a very different world.

Temptations

There are days when the work we do for God is so steady that we do not look around. We serve without interruption, giving little thought to the bigger canvas on which God uses us to paint His story of renewal.

Sometimes we work very hard for long periods and during these periods God gives us all that we need to persist in His service. We have, during these periods of intensive service, little time to examine why we are serving God or what else we could be doing. We simply work. All is well. During these periods, God often withholds temptations of the more sublime variety, the "Do I really want to remain on this current course?" temptations. We barrel through the work, and God flows through us mightily even though we can be largely unaware of this. After a time, we get tired. Then comes a natural break. This can come in the form of an in-between period, or it is a time-off period. Perhaps we suffer with illness or a transition of service occurs. At those times, the floodgates can open.

God then allows us to struggle with the temptations necessary to secure our future service. The story with holiness, while written in the present, is concluded in the future. In other words, the end of the story is directly correlated to the action of the present. What will the end look like? That depends on what we choose today. The struggle we all experience of revulsion for the work that God wills for us is part of the work.

A farmer ploughing his field loves to reap what he has sown, yes, and this is good. He is getting it done. For us, I think we will rejoice when we can be like the farmer for whom one day is exactly like the next. He is as joyful turning over new ground as he is when taking in a harvest. It is about the movement, the service, regardless of what that movement or service is on any given day.

That stated, there are times of natural joy. Now we must all pause. An apostle working hard for Jesus has to think for a moment. What time of natural joy is there? It all appears to be hard work. And yet, the joy is in that very hard work. The amount of straining necessary on a given day becomes irrelevant. There is joy both on the hard days and on the easier days. There is joy on the days when the harvest seems to be coming in and when the seeds are only being put down. There is joy on the days of hail storms and killing frosts as well as the days on which little work is necessary because the sun and warmth seem to be doing all that is necessary for the field assigned to this farmer. In this case, I think we are examining a very experienced farmer indeed. The seasons come and go and the work of the day is the work of the day. He spends no time wondering whether or not he should have been a farmer. He *is* a farmer and this is his field. He will farm until he dies and the challenges and discouragements of one day are allowed to melt into the joys and encouragements of another day with little or no excitement.

We need to be calm surveyors of our life during the off times lest the enemy lead us into rebellion and danger. During the times when we are off, down or ill, let us examine both the canvas as a whole and then our little place on it with certainty that without us something would be missing. Let us, during these times of break, expect to struggle with temptations of the more sublime variety. Let us, as apostles, see these temptations coming.

To distinguish, between temptations and healthy general life scrutiny, I reference interior condition. Healthy general life scrutiny will include a calm interior which sits with heaven peacefully, mindful of heaven's unity with us as a created one. Temptations include the opposite of this. There is discomfort, interior itchiness and irritation, possibly anger, even panic and a feeling of wanting to escape from service as though the service were a prison or a quagmire or quicksand. Service to Jesus will not be like this. We will always have the choice. It is not a sand trap. We can turn away from Christ. Many have and many do and perhaps we will turn away from Christ ten times before Christmas. Who can say? But when the work lets up for a period of rest, reflection or change, the wise apostle will be alert to temptation.

November 19, 2009

Temptation can be a violent experience. It is difficult to write about the more violent temptations because they are so personal. By personal, I do not mean embarrassing but rather designed to upset the individual. What would upset one person would barely impact another and what would put the other person into an emotional tailspin would barely register on the first apostle. For example, one person could be sent into the greatest upset by the disorder of a room. Another would throw himself happily onto the nearest chair and enter into the disorder, finding it relaxing. Also, temptations can alter in intensity from one day to the next. For example, on one day, disorder could be soothing on the same person and on the next day the same disorder could be experienced as unsettling. What we can count on is that periods of temptation will come and they will go.

The goal for us must be to navigate these periods without doing damage to God's plan or hurting the people around us. It must be helpful to make acts of love for those around us. We accept the humanity of others as Jesus accepts our humanity. When others react to us badly, we accept this as inevitable. We check ourselves in terms of actions and disposition and then accept that we have done our best. Now I will state again that the key to all of this is interior disposition. If we are calm in examining ourselves, this is a good thing because we cannot do an accurate examination of our disposition when we are agitated and upset. Clearly, the upset indicates a risky disposition and is, all by itself, a good indication that we are either at risk of making judgment errors or at risk of being unjust to others.

Where there is objective slight from another, meaning that any reasonable person would agree that another behaved badly toward us, we accept that hurt will be present. This hurt can make it difficult to deal with the person in the moment. Perhaps it is wiser to allow some time to elapse so that we can examine the events which may have prompted the hurtful behavior. If, upon reflection, we feel it is helpful, we must approach the person in honesty and explain our experience. Many things can be accepted if there is humility. It might be helpful to think in terms of the benefit to an ongoing relationship. If we are not involved in a relationship with someone that requires a continual flow of grace, perhaps it is better not to engage in an attempt to resolve conflict. We should be careful in considering which relationships will benefit from the hard work of honest exchange. Often a wise apostle will deem it pointless to put their wound on the table for examination. Often, common sense will prompt one to expose the wound only to Jesus for healing. There is no point in conflict for the sake of conflict and it is best to minimize drama.

Oh dear, I am going to get into deep water and yet I feel I must. Some people are *always* resolving conflicts and *always* examining interactions. This is a serious distraction. If I find that in a given relationship there is too much talk about the relationship, I begin to doubt whether or not the relationship is God's plan. Some things are just too much work and that tells me the whole thing could be a distraction. I am not referring to immediate family relationships. Those relationships are hard work at times and people make more mistakes doing no work than too much work in families. Even there, if someone is dragging another into constant fruitless dialogue about small issues and how they feel about them, also, if in these dialogues one person has more power, does most of the talking and the other does not feel free to express his or her feelings, then there is trouble.

I am talking about temptation and temptations come in many packages, often disguised, so it is good to pull the covers from them wherever we find them.

Temptations can be childish as in "I would like to kick this door that is stuck (or computer)," and they can be more sophisticated as in "I would like to leave this well-discerned vocation." They can be spontaneous as in, "Suddenly I feel like I do not want to go to work," or they can build over time as in "This person has been getting on my nerves for months and now I've had it." Temptations can be ridiculously easy to discern as wrong such as

"I think I would like to have sex with this person to whom I am not married," or they can be more confusing such as "I think I will stay in this damaging relationship because I'm afraid of what the person will do if I end it."

Temptations will always come where there is authority. One would think we would see these coming, they are so predictable. Everyone seems to know better than the one Jesus puts in charge. How can that be? It cannot be, really, so it must be us. Yes, those in charge will get it wrong at times. They will make mistakes, as we do. Yet, if they are the rightful authority, we, who are charged with submitting to their authority, must seek to protect them. This is so important in religious life but also in every life. The fact that the superiors in our lives are human gives us a steady stream of opportunity for assisting them and humbling ourselves rather than being the right to their wrongs and pulling against their leadership. Perhaps I have beaten this one to death or, more likely, Jesus likes it repeated as it is so important for unity.

Temptations. We could never be finished. In counselling each other, it is good to be aware that we cannot discount something in a friend because it would not tempt us. In other words, it is often the case that we laugh off the temptations of a friend because we ourselves would have no trouble resisting such inspirations. But we must not do this. If someone brings a temptation to us in conversation either casual or serious, we must assess their danger with them. We must stop the conversation and remark upon their struggle so they themselves will not take it lightly and they themselves will be prompted to examine their danger, if in fact there is any danger.

Clearly, we can all be guilty of throwaway comments when we are angry. Every mother has heard statements like these from her children. Possibly every child at some time will say, "I hate my brother (or sister or even parents)." We would be tedious friends indeed if we called our companions to examine every statement they made. But as apostles we should be alert to temptation themes in ourselves or others.

November 20, 2009

In our human existence, we will experience injustice. What greater temptation to bitterness than to be misjudged and wrongly condemned? Who has not at some time been the victim of condemnation and shame? The obvious must be stated and that it is this was the Lord's experience so we, as Christians, will all have some share in this if we follow Him. But to examine temptation, let us recognize the truth which is that we often hold the flashlight which sheds the harsh light of Satan on others.

People look different when we are looking at them through the eyes of Christ than they do when we look at them through the eyes of the enemy of Christ. God's eyes will always look compassionately on a person. This does not mean that Christ's eyes are blinded to truth. On the contrary, it is perfect truth to say that the eyes of the Savior view with complete truth. We can be observers of those around us and also be compassionate, keeping the flaws of others in perspective.

Immature spirituality focuses on sin, sin and more sin. All day long, the newcomer thinks about sin, in himself and others. Now when a person is learning a new sport, the rules are explained to him and the novice begins participation by trying not to break the rules. There is no other way. If you do not learn the rules, you cannot play the game with any success. But this must eventually blend into a more advanced performance where the athlete is freed from the constant worry about breaking the rules as he rises to a level of participation where he experiences the beauty of the sport.

To make this perfectly clear, a person learning to play basketball initially must make an effort to stand outside of the out of bounds line when throwing the ball in to his teammate. This absorbs his attention because he does not want to make a mistake that would jeopardize his success. But after weeks of practice, the player stops thinking about this out of bounds line and stands behind it automatically, which leaves him free to concentrate on more important things, like where he will throw the ball, who is the correct receiver of the ball and how he should outsmart or avoid the enemy standing in front of him.

The newer player will barely be aware of the opposition in front of him because he is so concentrated on not stepping over the line. He is largely unaware of his teammates. During the game, he is acutely sensitive to where the feet of others are placed as he studies the line rule and he can often be seen sending out a forceful outcry when he notices violations on the part of others. He is as harsh with others as himself.

I think the coach would say to these new players, "Well done. You are doing an excellent job of staying behind the line. Now let's think about how you are going to move around on the court." He is trying to draw the player into the more advanced theory of the game.

In some cases, the players do not seem to advance. Perhaps they are afraid. We will avoid discussion of the why right now. What is true is that you can have a new player holding the ball under his arm, pointing constantly to his feet and how 'safely' they are placed and then pointing out the past and present violations of the other players on the court. The coach in vain attempts to lure the player into letting the game begin. Other players become frustrated, fearfully checking their footing. Nobody is really playing the game. They have become like robots, simply on the court trying to avoid mistakes.

This player is missing the point, literally in basketball, but figuratively in the spiritual life. The beauty of the game is the interplay between the players, the poetry of the movement toward the destination as the ball is passed back and forth and protected from the 'bad' agenda of the opponents who will interfere with the goal which is to score a basket. When the basket is scored there is a rush of satisfaction amongst the team but little or no pause for congratulations because the game continues.

Sometimes a newer player who has absorbed the spirit of the game will make a valiant run, violating many rules but executing his own version of a perfect score. The good coach will admire the style and see what hope the future holds for this player because, despite his unintentional violations, this new player truly shows aptitude for embracing the beauty of the sport.

The immature player will not acknowledge the aptitude of the newcomer. He will be stuck at the first violation of the player and miss the beauty of the execution. He will then list the violations. The coach, conversely, rejoices with the one who shows high aptitude and says to him, "Wonderful. Magnificent offering! Let's do it again now and try to avoid a few things."

What will the coach do with the players who cannot get past foot placement? I think he will put them on the sideline doing drills. What else can he do? These players do not advance. They have trouble working with a team and they are too hung up on the little rules to get out there and actually play the game.

But they are on the team and because of this they are in the game, even if from the sidelines. They have shown up to play and are possibly a little relieved that they are not being put in. There is hope that they will, by watching the players on the court, eventually grasp the real point of the game and be less afraid of their mistakes. And it must be said that there are people in worse shape. Those would include some of the ones in the bleachers.

Ah…yes, the bleachers. What are these people doing?

They are studying the game for different reasons. Some like to watch so they can pick a side and be identified with it. Some show up to critique the performance of others and some spend the whole game shouting insults and baiting the players and the referees. The first two groups are valid observers with no hostility. They value the game and someday will probably participate.

The third group is disturbed. They hate the game and the players and they use the excuse of the game to spew their jealousy and bitterness out into existence as it relieves them from the constant suffering of it they feel inside. Sad, but always one is hopeful.

The game I am referring to is the holiness game and in this game everyone is welcome to play. The spirit of the game, the beauty, the advanced theory is love and the baskets are scored when the team works together and through love something beautiful comes into the world. This can be big, such as 38,000 orphans fed through the cooperation of a 'team', or it can be small, such as a teenager feeling valued through the compassionate listening of another. Each basket is a score for heaven and the little ones are hugely important and lead to the bigger ones in that if a boy or girl experiences love, he or she might go on to do great things with that love, even perhaps, feed 38,000 orphans.

We factor in the strengths and handicaps of each person and we have a glorious mix of capabilities and who watching basketball has not seen the worst player on the team come in from the sidelines and score the winning basket? It happens more than rarely and it gives us all thrills of joy. Perhaps the best players move up and down the court taking the most abuse because they are able for it. They have the advantage of the gift of understanding the theory of the game combined with the gift of possessing the physical ability. They have their weak points too, of course, and superiority and pride would be a serious risk for them.

The foot placement obsession referenced is the obsession with sin. This is a temptation to miss the whole point of the game. This is the immature spirituality that is so focused on the rules that it cannot see the point of the rules which is to provide an orderly and safe framework within which to play the game.

I am not saying to break the rules. One cannot be a good player if one is always breaking rules. But there are times when someone is knocked out of bounds or falls out of bounds. If he had been better, would he have managed not to fall out of bounds? I do not know but the reality is that it is unrealistic to expect that players will never make mistakes. And often those who think they are the referees do not see the fouls suffered by the ones who get knocked out of bounds.

Yes, everybody falls out of bounds or puts his foot over the line at some point. This is inevitable. So there should be no excitement about this fact. It is part of the game. The key is that we get back on the court and keep passing the ball to others and catching it when it comes to us. Giving love and receiving love. We will not have forever to play. Every game ends. And players will change.

November 23, 2009

It is true that often someone experiencing an intense period of play will be exhausted. That exhaustion will manifest itself in different ways but if we consider a sport, any sport, and think of a player who has just exerted himself heavily, we will picture a person who looks exhausted. How will this person behave? Perhaps, he will not behave as the best version of himself. Often a coach will observe signs of fatigue and pull a player out to rest.

Jesus does this also, as He knows that there are times when we need to sit out for a time. We must be very careful how we view someone who is either exhausted or resting and we must be very careful to identify the need for rest in each other.

Truly, temptation is our reality. If a person found himself on a desert island, he would experience temptation. He would be tempted to fail in trust, tempted to despair perhaps and possibly tempted to anger or bitterness. Why is he stuck on the island? Why are not others stuck on the island? Whose fault is it that he is on the island and why isn't his island as pretty as the island of others? These are the barest few temptations.

Next, add fifty more people to the island and tell the person he has to live and work with them. Oh my, the possibilities for temptation might become far more numerous. So it must be true that while working with others can provide us with different temptations, we cannot blame others because even without them there would be temptation.

Now, perhaps a person might think that they are better off being alone. This is true, if that is what God wills. But most people are called to deal with temptations as they work alongside others. It is clear that God needs relationships to work and to be holy. Each person must be tireless in combating temptation because a plan is at stake, a given course desired by God for the kingdom. This could be a marriage, a superior and charge or a parent/child relationship. It could be a friendship. It could be anything. Look at God's work and the possibilities are endless in terms of what God achieves through the relationships in our lives as well as, at times, interactions between strangers.

We spend so much time in our own heads. We think of whispers from the cross, that is, those whispers coming from Jesus, urging us to be tolerant and holy, as opposed to whispers from hell, that is, those whispers urging us to be bitter and selfish. As we said, the enemy tries to show us the worst possible motives present in those around us. The enemy tries to highlight all that is dark about humanity and while it is true that those around us could be tempted to sin and bitterness, it is also true that in many cases those around us understand the author of their thoughts and rebuke temptations to abuse their power over us, emotionally or practically. We can see bad symptoms sometimes and become alarmed, but we must pray for those with whom we serve and trust the Lord to help them. This is so important.

Someone once reported a dream. In the dream a large snake coiled itself around the person. Whenever anyone looked at the person, all they saw was the snake. It was clear that the person was not the snake and yet the snake distracted people from the person, drawing their eyes to himself and his putrid coils. Because the snake had snugged itself up so closely to the person, people had difficulty differentiating one from the other.

We must be very careful not to do this to anyone.

To clarify, we must not allow Satan to persuade us that the people around us are like him. Satan will always try to destroy what is good and holy. He will try to tempt us against each other. He will try to persuade us that we are being treated badly or worse than we are or that we are owed something from someone that they either cannot give or do not understand that they owe or that they do not even possess. I am searching and hoping to land, randomly if necessary, on the way the devil works against God's willed relationships. How often have we worked ourselves into a full fledged war against someone only to find out that the person never fired the first shot?

I am talking about misunderstandings and assumptions. For example, a person says something. We later wonder what the person *meant*. We can ascribe good intentions or bad, hostility or affection. We can make a decision to say, "I am not sure so I will not worry," leaving it to the other to communicate more clearly if necessary, or we can let the enemy take us to all manner of outrage and defensiveness over what we *think* the other meant. What a waste of time and energy and yet, this is the difficulty we have in both dealing with others and concentrating on Christ.

Clear communication is a heavenly grace and it can be acquired if people are willing to be humble. This type of heavenly communication requires hard work and self-evaluation. How grateful God is when He observes two people trying to get it right for Him in this regard. This communication is part of the reverence God asks us to have for each other. If we desire a holy relationship, we will work for an honest relationship. If we desire to protect God's will, we will be willing to work at the relationships God wills. Everything else is shadow boxing, positioning, power mongering. Who needs it? Not God's holy apostles.

Being continually misjudged while searching for God's will in a relationship can be painful but, as time goes by, the holy apostle sees that others will eventually recognize God's presence in their interactions. "Time makes more converts than reason", as Thomas Paine said. At the very least, it can be trusted that all will be known in heaven.

November 25, 2009

We must all be alert to the more or less constant presence of temptation in our lives. Rarely will there be complete absence of struggle and each suffering brings its own temptations. Often, when we are sick, we suffer not only physical illness but many other forms of temptation. For example, during one recent fact finding mission, I asked those around me how the enemy was tempting them. Initially, each said they were not being tempted. Here is an example of a closer look:

"How is the enemy tempting you today?"

"He's leaving me alone today, thank God."

"Are you sure?"

"Yes, I think so. No temptations today."

"Nothing is disturbing your peace?"

"No."

"Nothing is making you anxious?"

A slight pause.

"Indigestion. The enemy is getting me with indigestion."

Now, at first glance, this seems laughable and ridiculous. How can the enemy use indigestion to tempt someone? But as the woman went on, this is the story that emerged.

"Last evening I went out to eat. Later, I began to feel terrible indigestion. I was alone and thought about dying. What if it was a heart attack and I was by myself? Who would I call? What if the phone was broken? Then I wondered if I had made enough preparations for my funeral. What if the children began to fight because I had not organized my affairs? I began to worry about my affairs then and also what would happen to my obligations. I felt sure it was cancer and wondered how long I had to live. I knew a woman who had indigestion, which was diagnosed as cancer and she was dead in three weeks. What if I only had three weeks? Could I get organized in time? I pulled out some bank statements to check my savings. Finally, exhausted with this, I went to bed where I worried for most of the night."

Clearly, in moments such as this, an act of trust in God can restore peace. Perhaps this act must be repeated and repeated as Saint Faustina urges us throughout her writings. If we have a little trust in God, we must thank Him and ask for more. If we have a lot of trust in God, we must thank Him and ask for trust for others. If we have no trust in God, we must tell Him we need help immediately.

"Is anything else tempting you?"

"No. Nothing."

"Are you mad at anyone from the past? Is there anything from the past that hurts?"

Suddenly, tears welled up and she began to recount a situation from long ago where she had been hurt. This caused a serious temptation to bitterness and upon closer inspection it was clear that she needed God's help with this.

"Is anyone bothering you now? Anyone getting on your nerves or making you feel sad?"

Out came a current situation where a person had evidently done something hurtful. Upon examination, it came to light that a complete and total misunderstanding had occurred with absolutely no malice on the part of the other person. She was fighting windmills in this regard but being badly tempted to anger and hurt.

"How is your prayer life? Are you happy enough with it?"

A deep sigh.

"I'm sure God would rather I didn't go in to pray half the time. I can't concentrate. I think I am useless in terms of prayer. I often wonder if I'll even make it to heaven with what goes on in my head."

Clearly this could not be accurate. This was a dedicated lay apostle. Sometimes we do not separate temptation from sin. We can all be tempted to bitter, destructive or sexually inappropriate thoughts. The thoughts alone do not constitute a deliberate departure from God's will and it must be said that this woman was a committed prayer person and daily communicant. Yet she was so hard on herself.

These were whispers from the enemy of peace. Jesus, if allowed, would whisper words of consolation and calm, urge to forgive and give words of companionship and love. Jesus would encourage and direct, console and guide.

We must try to be aware of where to look for the day's temptations and bring the situations to Jesus for light and healing graces. Jesus will give us the grace to deal with all of these temptations if we allow Him. We want to keep our eyes on Christ but watch out for holes in the road.

To believe the enemy is not tempting us is to be tricked.

During this study of temptation, it became clear that some apostles were better than others at shutting windows of temptation. One young women, when asked if she felt concern about her spiritual condition replied, "Oh no. I'm not worried about that at all. The priest in Confession told me I was doing fine and that I should be patient with myself. If he thinks I'm doing okay, I must be."

This uncomplicated view of a soul's own condition is a good one to model oneself on. It must be said that this young woman was behaving in a holy manner and yet she was not in denial about any sins she was committing. She was simply calm about her imperfection and prayer life. She would be the first to identify areas where she needed to improve but there was a spirit of self-respect and tolerance for others as opposed to self-condemnation and judgment of others. She was confident about God's presence in her soul.

It must be good to assume that the enemy of peace would like to disrupt the holy relationships in our lives. He is the Great Contaminator.

Someone could say, while standing in front of your house, "The sky is gray". The enemy would whisper, "He thinks it is your fault the sky is gray. He is mad at you. He feels superior to you because the sky is blue over his house. You shouldn't have to take this from him. Who does he think he is telling you the sky is gray? He's going to hate you because the sky is gray." One could go on endlessly. One could get more serious about the statement, but it is best to choose the most innocuous statement in the world because it is not the statement or the circumstances, but what the Great Contaminator does with the statement and the circumstances. And it is not the other person who is responsible for policing our thoughts, but we who must police our thoughts.

If the study of psychology has contributed to humanity, and of course it has, the greatest contribution must be that it encourages us to look inward and examine ourselves, our motives and our wounds, and integrate these internal processes and happenings to our external selves, meaning our daily walk and our relationships with those around us. It is so important to identify our 'stuff' and not put it on someone else. If someone attacks us without merit, it could be their struggle that prompts the attack. We have to learn to identify our fears and insecurities and how these fears and insecurities affect our heavenly obligation, which is to love. Clearly, if someone we love speaks we must listen and examine their observations but there are times when the enemy tempts those around us against us and there are times when the enemy tempts us against those around us.

To simplify, Jesus will always shine a light of compassion and truth on the people in our lives. The enemy will always shine a light of suspicion and anger on the people in our lives.

As Christ followers, we must look at the people in our lives in truth, with compassion. We can judge objective wrongs as wrongs and still view those acting out those wrongs with compassion. We can say, "Ah, yes, it is pain and vulnerability that prompts these bad actions against me." Viewed in this way, we can avoid bitterness and condemnation, even as we deal with the effects of the wounds inflicted by others.

We, committed to Christ and plugged into His constant healing graces, can stop the destruction from spreading and even push back at it by returning love for hostility.

Every apostle with experience has seen this work and we know that God is good. Simply put, His plan, modelled by His sacrifice in the Passion, holds water.

November 26, 2009

It seems there is a heavenly plan for each human interaction. This heavenly hope aims toward a holy outcome. God hopes that we will respond to everyone in our life with His love and further His plan. We, for whom God's plan is the mandate if we pledge our allegiance to Him, must think in terms of proceeding in our relationships in a heavenly ordered fashion.

Yes, our relationships must be ordered toward heaven's goals. What does that mean and why do I place this subject in a category entitled temptation? Well, because this is where we get into so many knots and jams. This is where humanity can do the most damage and inflict the most wounds.

There are big circles of service in which some people participate. These include governments, businesses and whole faith communities. The Church itself is a circle of service, possibly the biggest circle of service from heaven's perspective. Then there are smaller circles of service of which the aforementioned consist and which the heavenly kingdom is based upon.

Let us say that a circle of service is an invisible area of light wherein a person joins another person or persons for an interaction that God hopes will bring about a certain outcome. There are people we are called to work with and often when we encounter them, we feel a strange recognition, like a thrill of familiarity. Who has not met someone and felt completely drawn to them, as though perhaps we have known them before? We wonder to ourselves. We puzzle. We examine this draw and delight in it. Sometimes it is so strong it can bemuse us and startle us and make us suspicious.

And, as strongly as God connects us and seeks to order our relationship to His plan, the enemy seeks to sow disorder.

Ah the disorder. Songs and poems are written about this. One person loves, another rejects. One person rejects, another loves. One inflicts wounds, the other suffers. One suffers, the other inflicts wounds. Sometimes people collide like tectonic plates and mutually land so hard amidst the debris of the collision that they are stunned and forced to examine the reality of their behavior in the circle where they met.

Sometimes we feel an emotional attraction to those God desires us to work with and sometimes we do not. We have something to overcome in the last instance and something to protect in the first.

It must be said that both should result in the same end, meaning mutually loving and disciplined advancement into the service God has willed for the team He has assembled. The love should be the same in both instances. There should be concentration on the service God has willed. Both types of relationships should provide a degree of fellowship that is fruitful but firmly ordered toward the protection of each person in God's holy will.

This can be difficult to achieve but when it gets to the place God intends, it is so beautiful and life-giving and the circle of service, which includes the relationship between the people, becomes an oasis where each person or persons can come to be refreshed by God's love that flows between them. Such a gift! Such a foretaste of heaven! Truly, God reveals His nature in these interactions and the people involved are allowed to experience intimacy, which, as we said, takes place when two people meet to the accompaniment of grace.

Now, this type of heavenly love often befuddles us and can confuse us, particularly if God is inviting a man and woman into a circle of service that does not include marriage. The reason this confuses us is because the modern world has us convinced that *any* love between a man and woman, unless it is of the order of familial relationships, should end sexually. End is the operative word in this case because unless there is a sacramental union, marriage, physical sexual expression will risk killing the dignity and reducing the circle of service to ashes. This cannot be God's will, unless the graces of the Sacrament are present. It must always be categorized as a mistake. The physical sexual expression not willed by God then becomes something that the relationship must overcome as opposed to something that deepens and perpetuates the relationship.

History is rife with these types of mistakes, it is true, even amongst holy people. And the enemy is gleeful about these mistakes and tends to parade them wherever possible. The enemy hits these hard with floodlights because the greatest danger to Satan's plan is God's love between people serving on earth. God's love between people will bring them to a level of heroic sacrifice that includes death when necessary. Observe the greatest sacrifice, that is, the Passion and understand that actions that model themselves after this are also co-redemptive for mankind. This is why the enemy works tirelessly to distort, hitting love with gross distortion wherever it springs up.

There are many beautiful glimpses of heavenly love and many of God's children have sought to illuminate it. One such man is Fr. Maurice Reidy. In his book, *Freedom to be Friends*, he states it this way:

> *But in those distant moments before stars and galaxies were born, the weight and the volumes were just right, and here, millions of years further on, you exist and so do I.*

> *And what is it about the magic of a smile, or of a conversation, that provokes in me the alchemy of affection? Why is it that just these eyes speak to me, just this laughter, just these hands, these tears? What are the hidden impressions, belonging to a distant childhood perhaps, but still casting a long shadow or a shaft of light somewhere deep within, which are called up by them? What possibilities they conjure up, and what wants, yet these can be lost again and forgotten if the promise of love is not persevered with. The thrill of heart meeting heart is something like my very existence, it might never have happened, and its very happening is some kind of benediction.*

Oh, dear. It is so beautiful I get lost in it and forget my own thoughts. I cannot help but rejoice in such beauty. Truly, Jesus must have been at work when these words flowed from the hands of this man. You see, I believe that he is describing heavenly intimacy, such as the saints experience in heaven. He is describing the foretaste of heaven. Only in grace can moments such as the above occur. He references the risk of loss of God's plan when he notes that the 'promise of love is not persevered with'. The promise of love, I believe, is God's participation. If we take the relationship to a place of sin or mistake, literally thinking a 'miss take', meaning, we got it wrong or landed in the wrong destination, perhaps in sin, we in a sense break the promise of God's beautiful participation. We abandon God with each other, preferring our self-will, which, regardless of how we attempt to put wrapping paper and bows on it, is selfish.

In this time when the goal of chastity has been run out the door of many relationships, God's children search in vain for the delight, so sublimely described by Father Maurice Reidy. Somewhere inside, God's children know that this beautiful intimacy is their heavenly entitlement. They, in their fruitless searches, are doomed to disappointment and despair and transported over time to cynicism instead of the child-like innocence and joy willed by the Father.

What is the answer? Prayer. We must examine each of our relationships prayerfully. We must listen carefully to the whispers from the cross and be reverent about seeking God's will with each person in our lives. We must be rigorous in identifying self-will and selfish wants and overcome them with regard to the people God has chosen to send us.

In the same way, we must not capitulate to someone else's desires in the name of being selfless. On the contrary, we will sometimes have to keep our hand up to those around us as they will be inclined to bring their self-will into the circle of service and this self-will, while to be expected and compassionately viewed, cannot be entertained if God's plan is to be maintained. Yes, we are patient with the self-will of others even as we are patient with our own self-will but only through constant self-examination can our relationships be protected for Jesus and for heaven's scheduled renewal.

November 27, 2009

It would be easy enough to proceed into God's will with those involved in our given circles of service if everyone thought as we think. But not everyone is an apostle. It will often be the case where we are involved in a circle of service with someone who does not seek God's will. Sometimes, we are involved with people who feel hatred for us. This must be stated because it is accurate. Still, given each circumstance, there is a holy outcome which can be achieved if we, ourselves remain in the divine will.

For example, I often think of God's will in a situation where there is contention. At that time it helps to try to determine the best possible response, given God's presence in our soul. We might say, "What would a saint do? What is the holiest response? What then, will be the probable outcome?" There is great talk about tough love in this time and the reason for this is that people sometimes get away with a lot. Tough love, I think, must be the kind of love that says, you are no longer going to use me to do the wrong thing.

This is a good kind of love and it is right to categorize a mode of behavior as love, even though it described as tough. At first glance, the words *tough love* could be viewed as oxymoronic. Love is thought of as gentle and soft. But any parent knows that love that is too gentle and soft with children can lead to spoiled and unhappy children and often gentle and soft in love can mean taking the easy way out. Real love is willing to stand firm in what is right for the sake of the person one loves. Real love is willing to speak the truth, even when it will cause discomfort. Real love is committed to growth in a healthy direction for the relationships in one's life. Real love will engage in conflict without flinching. It is often said that the right thing to do is not necessarily the easy thing to do and never is this more apparent than with the people with whom we walk through life.

The holiest and most pure relationships will include misunderstanding and conflict while the people involved serve in exile from heaven.

There are close relationships and not-so-close relationships. It is important to Jesus that we discuss conflict because there is no need for misunderstanding or conflict to result in behavior that is not consistent with Christ's example as seen in Holy Scripture. How did Jesus behave when there was conflict? He spoke few words but they were true words. It is best, in the area of conflict, if we spend time going through a situation of difficulty in the presence of Jesus and conclude on a holy course of action. Anger makes this even more necessary because anger leads to the enemy's plan. People love to talk about righteous anger and so often refer to the Lord's behavior in the temple. We like to convince ourselves that our anger is righteous. I am equally convinced that rarely will our anger be righteous. More often it will be plain old self- indulgent anger which is symptomatic of pride. I speak as an experienced person, not an observer, and I can assure the reader that Jesus would like us to avoid acting in anger whenever possible.

Humility allows for wounds. This is partially why humility is so important. If a person is humble, he will be willing to say, "I am hurt." When we admit something has hurt us, we can steer away from anger and take things calmly, acting with Christ to deal with any misfires in the relationships around us. This calm course will help us to remain an asset to heaven as opposed to a liability.

It must be noted that Jesus, in Holy Scripture, acted consistently with kindness, gentleness and humility. Jesus was continually misjudged and maligned. He returned love for hostility. It would be an excellent exercise for us to spend some time today thinking of who in our day is hostile to us and how we will follow the Lord's example as set out in Holy Scripture and treat these people with patience and kindness. Let us look, not at the Lord's righteous anger in one example, but at the Lord's parade of loving acceptance for those with whom He served.

This method of behavior, rejecting anger in favor of humility, becomes habit forming. How beautiful it is to witness someone who has gained mastery over himself in this way. Their rare departures into anger or thoughtless remarks are reassuring in terms of their humanity but also stark contrasts from their normal behavior. It is good to see what a person could look like if he allowed himself the self-indulgence of anger because through these little glimpses, we can appreciate more fully their beauty in heavenly self-control. We can see it in ourselves and say, "My goodness, I do not look my best in this situation. I must work harder to gain mastery over myself."

Oh dear. Some personalities and some biochemistries will have great difficulty here. So be it. In our patience we will possess our souls and that is our hope. Better to find oneself in a garden full of weeds holding a shovel than find oneself in a garden full of weeds attempting to call the weeds flowers. We know the truth. We know what God is asking. He wants us to try to conduct ourselves as He would with each other so we set off on a path of improvement, each day and every day.

December 10, 2009

It is clear that the more closely connected we become to Christ in us, the more closely we project an accurate communication of our true self. Our true self, created by God, merges into God and we reflect God's intent. Imagine a pot with one healthy flourishing flower, a hyacinth, for those who like clear imagery. Imagine this flower having the perfect nutrients in the soil, the perfect amount of light and water and the perfect quality of environs, meaning not too hot and not too cold. This is an ideal image, and crossing over a bridge to humanity, unrealistic.

But to follow it down, this hyacinth projects a presence that is the ideal plan for a hyacinth bulb in that it has received the best possible circumstances and it has duly flourished. Sometimes, all around a flower bulb can seem ideal and yet some flaw, some biochemical happening, results in a bloom that is half-hearted or in a bulb that never blooms. The promise of a bloom, with the right circumstances, does not always result in what we expect and there is disappointment.

But it is too soon to talk about disappointment when we are admiring what appears to be the perfect outcome of the plan for the bulb. Such a scent is given off by this flower! One is hard put to smell this scent and not find his heart transported to a good place. We can say that the fully blooming hyacinth accurately reflects God's plan for the bulb.

In the same way, there are people who absorb what is good. With it they advance into Christ within and become the most beautiful examples of the Creator united with the created. I believe that they have an ability to use what is good to the fullest extent, absorbing the best possible benefit from all around them that is life-giving. These people also can flourish in the most arid circumstances because they seem to be oblivious to what is poisonous to others. They are hardy specimens and continually turn their faces away from what is contaminating, absorbing instead what is good. Where is the light? You will find these people facing it, even if it is only the smallest sliver of light. It is for this reason that people became joyous saints in concentration camps and prisons and it is for this reason that people become startling showcases of chastity in cultures saturated with impurity.

Some people project Christ regardless of what is happening around them.

Why is this? Well, I do not know. But I have an idea. I think that some remain very close to Christ within them. When a child is hiking with a party in the forest, the children are instructed in advance that in the event they become lost, they should stay in one place. This avoids the unfortunate possibility of both searchers and lost hiker continually avoiding each other through constant movement. The children are told, "If you get lost, hug a tree and wait for help."

In the same way, through life's trials and upheavals, life's pains and wounds and travails and traumas, if we are always touching God within us, we will be able to remain what we are intended to be, fully ourselves and projecting our unique goodness into the world for God. We have to hug God, keeping our arms wrapped around Him. God will not let go or move. It will be we who move away, sadly looking back at what God intended us to be.

What lures us away?

Temptation, of course. We are tempted away. We are drawn away. We are called out into danger and the further away we get from the base, that is, God within, the less we resemble our true selves. A mother looks at a child who is throwing a tantrum and making a complete spectacle of himself and shakes her head sadly. She, of all people in the world, knows that this is not her son. She might even say, "He's not himself." Clearly not, he is someone odious to others, someone who hurts and offends and who is unwilling to accept the life-giving love of those around him who would minister to him and help him learn to absorb the nutrients from the love that God has willed for him and provided for him.

I hear the cries of those who say, "Environment, physiology, traumatic wounding, he is not responsible." This is true, of course, and physiology, psychology and theology are married in heaven. Why wouldn't they be? They are all part of the same truth and truth cannot contradict itself. If truth seems to contradict itself, we have either untruth or limited understanding of truth.

I see a woman. She is so beautiful, so feminine in her heart and her heart united to God is glorious to behold. She projects this to others, of course, but it is so hesitant, so halting. And yet, she is a triumph because she has overcome so many temptations. She has rejected worldly notions and worldly responses to her pain. Truly, the world would justify her if she would only offer her pain for the soothing voice of the tempter. The tempter could then seduce her further, out further away from God within. The further away he drew her, the less she would look like herself. As it stands, given that she has closed many windows and most drafts and worldly breezes cannot draw her, we have Goodness evident through her. And yet, there is a handicap.

The handicap is the remaining temptation to reject God's goodness within. The tempter, raging against the closed windows, hisses and whispers, "You are still not good enough." By rejecting God's goodness within, she limits the amount of intimacy that is available to her. Shall we call this low self-esteem? I do not know. What is clear is that we have a functioning Christian, serving well, but one who is extremely hurtful to those closest to her because in rejecting her own goodness, that is, the true goodness of God within, she retains a kernel of bitterness which limits her in intimacy. Those closest to her, if they are good, will see the goodness and the desire for goodness and while they lament the coldness and mistrust, they will consistently offer light in the hope that eventually, through an action of grace, she will begin to absorb what is life- giving from their love.

Such wounding. Such ripple effects. Such generational implication. When we reject the opportunities to perfect ourselves, we are rejecting goodness, not just for us, but for so many others with whom we are called to serve. We are rejecting goodness, not just for the present, but for the future, our future and the future of others. And when we embrace the opportunities to perfect ourselves, we are embracing goodness, not just for ourselves, but for so many others and not just for the present, but for the future. If all is the eternal present, and it is, one action of goodness today immediately impacts the world. The connectivity of the Body of Christ insures this.

Such high thoughts we are called to entertain as we serve scrubbing floors and digging holes. Scrubbing floors and digging holes is my euphemism for all of God's good work that we toil at each day.

We remember that sin first wounds the sinner and then moves with great determination out into the world to do additional damage. So we have the exquisite wounding of sin which stings the whole Body of Christ, having first stung the sinner, and then we have the polar opposite, the exquisite benediction of an act of goodness which blesses the whole Body of Christ, having first blessed the little saint-in-waiting. Through goodness comes healing for the person acting in goodness and for the whole of God's creation.

What we do, counts!

Goodness is self-perpetuating in that one act of goodness quickly gathers itself up and without hesitation rushes out into the world, to heal, to provide redress and to multiply. Goodness absorbs impurely motivated actions and sucks out any shred of purity to make itself grow. Goodness becomes formidable quite soon in that she is irresistible and soothing in her pure calming way, drawing all who encounter her back to their base, the safety of the tree where others can find them. You see, if a person has been drawn away from their base, they project a false self which confuses those closest to them because it is not real. Those not so close to them will interact fine and perhaps even admire and exult in the false self, possibly contributing to the creation of a superiority addict, but those closest, who are entitled to pure love, will be disappointed. God is in all of this and all is a process. We are called to find in each other what most resembles God, that is, His intent for each of us. By focusing on that, we can love those in our lives who hurt us.

Betrayal

There is something beautiful about betrayal. It can be an exquisite thing, a breath-stopping moment for an apostle. The reason betrayal can be exquisite is because it is a 'call to follow' of the highest order.

How did Jesus handle betrayal? Jesus handled it like a lamb. This does not mean that He was not tempted to bitterness but we know that He successfully overcame these temptations because one of his last statements was a plea for the Father to forgive those who were hurting Him. We must do the same. The reason a moment of betrayal must be breath-stopping is because in every betrayal the enemy has seeded a plan of destruction. At the very least, the enemy hopes to destroy our peace. At the very most, the enemy hopes for alteration of a heavenly plan. If our breath stops in the face of a betrayal, let that be a good thing because we want to move oh-so-carefully. We want to examine each possible course of action and separate our personal reaction from the response God should be able to expect from a holy apostle.

In the course of each life, we can expect to be betrayed. We can expect others to turn against us and be false, even perhaps while they pretend to be our friends. Falseness hurts the most. A proclaimed enemy at least allows us to be on guard. When one pretends to be a friend, we allow love to flow through us to them. We give. Our guard is down. When this love is exploited and it is found that person has abused love, one's trust can be badly shaken. Such hurt. The only place to take it is to the foot of the Crucified Christ. That is the only place where it will make sense. And, when we deliver this hurt to Jesus, He is able to console us and guide us through the temptations that accompany betrayal.

Now, there can be a grave temptation to slap back. This is a grave temptation for many reasons, the first and most being that we will do further injury to God's plan if we behave like God's enemy. Should we verbalize our hurt? Only if there is a receptivity at the other end. If there is no such receptivity, we risk engaging in what can become a dark dialogue that will take us further and further from peace. If there is receptivity, then we should verbalize our pain and seek reconciliation, but not until we are recollected in God's love. There is no benefit to taking anger, fueled by God's enemy, to someone who has hurt us. This is terribly sad and usually results in further damage to ourselves and the other party. Anger should be viewed as a temptation at all times, even when it feels righteous.

I see this struggle as beautiful because in it is buried the goal of perfection. If our call is to return love for hostility, then conditions of betrayal would provide for us optimal circumstances to do so. The head of Jesus is hanging down on the cross. He has given everything. He is finished. The journey has been successfully traversed. Jesus has accepted betrayal and returned love. "Father, forgive them for they know not what they do." Jesus allows compassion to react, not anger. May He give us all such richness in our service and may we each accept the graces to respond to betrayal as He did.

So it might be worthy of consideration that humanity should be suspicious of his first response until each person is well-trained in putting on the mind of Christ. Our first response will usually be generated by our humanity or the instinct of self. We must become adept at overriding this first response and inserting, instead, a second and hopefully more worthy response.

We are apostles. We are called to be messengers, envoys. We represent Jesus, not our weak humanity. When we feel betrayed, we are never in a better position to bring Christ to the world. As representatives of Jesus, we are watched, be assured. Others will want to see how we are going to act in conditions of duress. Think of Scripture. The apostles rejoiced at persecution. Do we rejoice at persecution? Much of this has to do with the old, faithful spiritual goal which is trust in God. We can find ourselves objecting strenuously saying, "I'm concerned about God's plan being protected." As a wise man once told me, "The Lord can look after Himself." In other words, God is all powerful and He will not allow any attack, however grave, to interfere with His plan. If we are attacked to a degree that heaven's plan suffers, then it is not our affair. Often it will be our pride that is suffering, if truth be told.

What normally happens is that the enemy tries to tempt us to believe that God's plan is in jeopardy when, in fact, God's plan often includes persecutions for His faithful followers. Jesus, as teacher, allows 'training' for us. He gives us opportunities to learn about persecution in order to help us grow into more serious service. Imagine a soldier dressed and trained but completely inexperienced in battle. Is he the best one to handle a serious campaign? Isn't it true that a wise general will put a seasoned soldier into a serious situation as opposed to one who has no battle experience? We must never reject the beautiful lessons God wishes to teach us. We should instead view everything as training and tuition and accept that only through learning today's lesson will we be fit for tomorrow's service.

So expect persecutions. Expect lies to be told and distortions to erupt. Christ will never allow the enemy to overcome us! If we feel overcome, so be it. God is not overcome.

God's plan for Jesus was perfect and it included His Passion and death. What do we fear? Similar treatment? Think of our brothers, Saints Peter and Paul. They viewed such treatments as a privilege and so must we.

Picture a conversation with a woman who is a daily communicant. She evidences a good deal of holiness to those in the community. The name of another woman comes up in conversation and suddenly out flows a torrent of hatred. This daily communicant harbored jealousy and envy for years. Listening to the extent of this bitterness and condemnation is excruciating as it is cruel and devoid of dimension or reason.

One had to consider the stories about genocide in Rwanda which killed an enormous amount of people, neighbors and fellow citizens against each other. It had to be acknowledged that had the same thing occurred in this country, there would be fuel for similar assaults through the harboring of such long term envy and jealousy.

This is neither a happy observation nor a comfortable realization.

Apostles, we must be more vigilant. If we have *any* ill feeling toward another, we must do battle with it in the presence of Jesus, who loves us all. If we do not do this hard work in our heads, the enemy will keep these feelings 'on file' and open them at a given time when we will then become a danger to the divine will through our bitterness.

It must be said that it is shocking where the enemy can take us if we are not vigilant. It is as if we are at a train station and there are two trains. If we harbor ill will, envy, jealousy and anger, it is as if we are getting on the train that leads to darkness. We must think about this very carefully. The tracks only go in one direction and once this train leaves the station it becomes more and more difficult to get off. I think that if we were able to see where we were going by looking down the line of the railway tracks, we would immediately offer these things to the Lord for eradication and humble ourselves before Him.

We do not want to resemble Cain and Abel.

There is a train which goes in another direction and that leads to peace. When we covet the respect that another is given or the attention that is being paid to another then we are not reverencing what has been given to us. We then, if we get on the wrong train, will try to 'look' like them, stealing their identity, as it were and offering it to others falsely for the admiration we crave. This is not good modeling.

To say we admire the virtues in another and strive to acquire these same virtues is wonderful. To look at the virtues of another and to admire the attention these others may get because they possess these virtues, and to then try to 'steal' the virtues by mimicking them but not practicing them, is diabolical in nature. We do not lovingly try to live the same goodness. We, like the chameleon, try to become a similar color. We are not authentically ourselves in virtue. We are pretending to be someone else. We are away from our real identity with Christ. We are projecting ourselves somewhere else, somewhere where we most certainly are not. The person, the source of our envy, becomes then a stinging reproach to us, a reminder of who we are not. And thus we see the birth of hatred. That person will be the one we betray.

Oh dear. It is so sinister in the final degree that we would ask God to keep us at the station and never let us go anywhere but that is not consistent with the free will we have been given. God wants children who choose Him freely. It is a problem and it is an old problem. These are the thieves and brigands who make war on God's children because they envy God's children.

The Stripping

Jesus is stripped of His garments.

Into the life of every follower of Christ will come an experience of stripping, when, through betrayal, humiliation, sorrow, suffering, loss, illness, or failure with consequences, we are forced to confront our selves.

To be specific, these experiences can happen when children gang up and reject another child, when someone is bullied or teased, when a person is fired from a job, when someone is sent to prison, or loses all of his money as in when a successful person must file for bankruptcy or when a bank repossesses a car or forecloses on a mortgage. Other examples include someone with an addiction being publicly exposed or placed into treatment, a spouse leaving one with consequent separation and divorce, unplanned pregnancies, unjust accusations, being victimized through rape or other assault or anything that includes deep disappointment in either another person or simply in life's circumstances. The death of the loved one or serious illness could be considered a stripping. Certainly though, into every life, will come some form of this experience.

In this stripping we are laid bare in a way that compels us to observe ourselves in truth. This can be traumatic but this experience also can be a powerful vehicle for advancement and growth, spiritually, mentally and psychologically. Only through examination of our true self will we find ourselves able to identify in us what is good, what is the product of our wounds and where we need healing.

There we find Christ, patiently waiting, hoping and alert.

While possibly experiencing searing pain, the one searching for his or her personal truth will come closer and closer to union with Christ. We cannot take all of the truth at once, one suspects, so in His mercy, God may allow a series of these stripping experiences suited to our strength in the areas mentioned. At some point on the journey, during one of the strippings, the searcher looks upon his essence with trembling eyes, expecting the usual shame and finds instead, calm. When this happens, the searcher is beginning a new process, one that ends in total liberation. The searcher is getting closer and closer to his core and is discovering in his essence, his true identity with God. Once this is achieved, no further serious stripping is necessary because only truth remains.

It is for this reason that the saints passed time in many types of prisons, physical, emotional and spiritual, peacefully and reflectively. They were laid bare with Christ and found it to be good! They, in their exposed humanity, found peace.

All thought of worldly approval must flee at this point. All outrage. All trepidation at the prospect of condemnation.

When a person has allowed the stripping and has cooperated willingly with the grace sent from heaven, the person gazes at his own humanity with the compassion and delight of the Father, the Creator.

Even while the person may experience continual pain at suffering and persecution, he receives it with gentleness and kindness to his humanity. In other words he is compassionate with himself and his human limitations rest easily upon his head and heart.

To clarify, dear apostles, this means that instead of going around and around on a track of self-hatred in our head, we allow for the difference between how we would like to behave and how we actually behave during a period of temptation.

Once we advance into a willingness to be stripped, suffering is never disconnected from spirituality. To be clear, a sufferer must be seeking truth. Not all sufferers are seeking truth. If the sufferer is not seeking the truth of his condition then the trials and tribulations, the pains and betrayals, will be nearly unbearable and may prompt a lashing out. Alas, the trials and tribulations, the pains and betrayals are unavoidable for humanity. If we lash out, we can miss the opportunity for examination of our essence, which, as stated, will eventually be a cause for delight.

At this core, where God and the searcher will eventually fuse, we have wonder, child-like hope and peace. But pain must come first where innocence is lacking, that is, in most of us. Who arrives at this core? Anyone who searches with a heart open to his human frailty. When will we arrive? We will arrive in God's good time if we are willing to self-examine in solitude.

The vertical relationship must be authentically sought. False piety always erupts in outrage because it seeks something other than holiness. Perhaps we must be both accepting of our limitations and eager to outpace them.

So, as the stripping advances, we become increasingly more comfortable with our core and we begin to spend more time there. Peace and integrity of mind come upon us. We begin to love ourselves in Christ's light, and instead of proceeding in fear of shame after experiencing weakness, we simply repent and seek to advance into virtue. Less and less can distraction snatch us away from self-examination. Less and less will conversation seem an attractive use of our time. We are at full surrender and those seeking to strip us for bad purpose are seeking to strip Christ Himself.

This core is a place of safety and for this reason the saints could accept death joyfully. It was all the same to them. They were proceeding into death, for them a place of perfect safety, from another place of perfect safety, that is, life.

Now, we must not be too disappointed if we cry out when we are stripped. We must view our condition realistically and accept that in our humanity we experience pain, much like an infant cries out instinctively when receiving an injection. Does the injection sting and leave a sore spot? Yes, but the sting in no way eradicates the truth which is that the injection brings with it hope for a greater good.

There is a sublime fruit that occurs naturally when we cooperate with Christ during these periods of intense purification. That fruit is the merciful and compassionate gaze that comes from the purified soul and seeks out others in love. The journey to holiness is really a journey to Christ. Only by accepting the compassion of the Savior for ourselves are we fit to lavish this compassion upon God's children.

Dear apostles, Jesus asks us to remain firmly fixed in the vertical relationship so that we can accept His healing and go on to help Him by flowing out to others. This is the road to renewal. We must journey to Christ as quickly as He wills by seeking greater virtue in every experience so that God can make us better and better conduits of His love.

With regard to the experiences of stripping we endure in life, if we want to become wise and holy, we will have to suffer the tuition.

The Stations of the Cross

1st Station- Jesus is condemned

The condemnation of Christ was anticipated, and was part, perhaps the greatest part, of God's plan for Jesus and for us. Tabor and Calvary. Transfiguration and Crucifixion. Both woven into the tapestry of the life of the Blameless One. Jesus was unjustly judged and condemned. When we share that experience, we must accept it quietly, like Christ.

2nd Station- Jesus accepts his cross

Accepting the cross is not a momentary action without consequences. It is a doorway through which we walk, entering an ongoing experience of Calvary as one who follows Christ.

3rd Station- Jesus falls the first time

Life throws us to the ground, whether through our own failures or the failures of others. This should not discourage us, even though discouragement accompanies the experience. Sometimes, even in the same day, following Christ requires a series of decisions to rise and continue on.

4th Station- Jesus meets his mother

Often our pain is increased by the reaction of others to our suffering. This painful prism of misunderstanding is another facet of the cross and should be viewed as such. Our Blessed Mother understands our pain perfectly, and just as she never left her Son, she will never leave us.

5th Station- Simon helps Jesus

We resemble Christ when we move to assist another who struggles to manage a cross and Christ Himself is pleased when we humble ourselves and accept the help of others.

6th Station- Veronica wipes the face of Jesus

We are prompted through charity and mercy to help others. Others are blessed and consoled. And we take away with us the imprint of God's goodness flowing through us, conforming us more completely to Jesus as He makes His way into the world.

7th Station- Jesus falls the second time

Oh sad disappointment! More pain. Still, the journey remains incomplete. Must we continue? We rise and return to the cross, to the plan unfulfilled.

8th Station- Jesus consoles the women of Jerusalem

Pity the women who share the dreadful concern of Mary for the children of God. Each person is someone's child and holds the hopes and prayers of a mother that the world will be gentle and kind. Oh Jesus, give us your mercy for others.

9th Station- Jesus falls the third time

The commitment is to the death. The Collapsed knows only that life remains and, as such, must be offered until it is exhausted. Up. Onward. God will sustain. Let the Spirit drive us forward.

10th Station- Jesus is stripped of His garments

How sublime is the offering of standing naked before those who hate us and yet, in some way, less cruel than standing stripped before those who love us. Oh Jesus, give us the trust to endure all humiliation with confidence in the ultimate triumph of God's love.

11th Station- Jesus is nailed to the Cross

Agony and relief. Total commitment leaves less room for question. We ask not 'if' anymore. We ask simply, 'how', moment by moment in life's anguish.

12th Station- Jesus dies on the Cross

Perseverance is the jewel of all jewels. Do not doubt the triumph. Do not back away from the course.

13th Station- Jesus is laid in the arms of His Mother

Quiet at last. A grief complete, but pregnant with joy. Humanity endures total stillness, even while time awaits the birth of all hope, the triumph of triumphs.

14th Station- Jesus is laid in the tomb

The body is reposed and the life is concluded, returned to timelessness once again.

Oh Jesus, help us to remember that the opportunity to serve you on earth will end. Give us the grace to be laid to rest after a life of offering, knowing that on each day we recognized you as our beloved King and lived, to the best of our ability, our allegiance to the Father. Give us the power of the Holy Spirit that we may continue to love in every circumstance life presents. Amen

Purity of the Church Visions

Purity of the Church Visions-a series of mystical
experiences recorded by Anne where she was shown the
Church in various circumstances at the direction of a heavenly
companion whom she refers to as her mystical friend.

September 8, 2008

I saw an area of fertile ground and suddenly I saw a wonderful green shoot emerge from it. The shoot grew steadily and it seemed that before my eyes it gave birth to more and more growth which eventually, quite spectacularly, came to be a beautiful hedge. I looked up from the hedge and saw that there had been other such shoots and from them also had grown, equally fast, the same hedges. The hedge itself was thick and verdant. The most beautiful blooms could be seen from which a fragrance of purity and heavenly scent came. I could see that the hedge was protective in nature, by its design, and that while it was absolutely beautiful, it was also impenetrable.

It is impenetrable because of heaven's power.

My mystical friend drew my eyes up and showed me a clear area in the middle of the border. I sensed it was the Church, which I know to be magnificent, but when I looked I was surprised. Inside the hedge was a Church, indeed, but it was a small, humble Church, such as one views in the countryside around Ireland. Far from being disappointed, I began to study this Church as it filled me with a feeling of dignity and peace. It was very clean and well-kept and I felt a strange wash of relief. The grounds leading to it were orderly and impeccably maintained. The paths leading to the various entries were generous and bordered by many different types of plants, all of which gave delight to me and to anyone who approached this Church. The sun on the stones of the Church provided continual warmth and light. The best word to describe this whole scene is purity.

Today, when the vision continued, I again admired the strength and beauty of the hedge and saw it as being constructed or produced from new outpourings of the Holy Spirit in the Church in the last period of time. These movements, new orders and so forth, will form and protectively surround the Church. My mystical friend asked me to examine the Church again and I marvelled at the beauty and strength of it. The roof was secure and

115

I could see that the windows were spotless and enabled anyone to view the inside of the Church, which I knew instinctively was as it should be. You could say that the windows provided outsiders with the ability to see that all on the inside was as clean and orderly as the outside. The windows were important.

My mystical friend asked me why this was different from the other Church. I said, "I have seen no other Church." Then, I saw another Church. It was a disturbing sight. There was no protective hedge around it. The hedge that had once been there was flattened and trampled. Nobody had kept it up or guided or nourished it. I saw this as a manpower problem as opposed to a malicious neglect. In the meantime, while this was happening, the building itself had gone to ruin. The roof was sagging, the windows were dirty and smudged so that nobody could see inside but really, a person would not want to walk inside this building as it looked structurally unsound. The terrible weeds had grown up all around the grounds and I saw that many were stinging nettles, which hurt people who tried to approach. No, this Church was neglected and sad. I couldn't bear this image. It hurt me. I felt no anger, only sorrow.

"What happened?" I asked.

"The disrepair occurred gradually, over time, as all such disrepair occurs. But there is hope."

At that moment, the Church changed and before me again I saw the beautiful Church. Such a relief! I studied it again and it struck me powerfully that this Church looked exactly like the buildings in heaven. It was pure and good and clean. Its lines were straight and its stones perfectly matched, creating patterns that were intricate but perfectly predictable when studied.

I remembered St. Francis being told to rebuild God's Church but there was something different and the word I use for this instruction was 'reclaim'. God is asking us to reclaim His Church and contribute to its repair and restoration.

When I studied the Church in the state of dreadful disrepair and neglect, I saw that the foundation was good, actually perfect, and that the stonework was sound and heavenly, which would make a new stone mason pause and admire the artistry of an old stone mason. I saw though that the perfection of the stone work or structure was obscured by a terrible mold that had spread across it, attaching itself and sucking strength from the masonry. This would have to be scraped off and then the stone treated. The old windows would have to come out, many were broken anyway, and this would be a hazardous job where people were likely to be hurt. Some pieces of glass came out easily; others were far more difficult to shift and actually had to be shattered and removed piece by piece. Again, this was going to be more time consuming than it looked at first glance.

When I studied the sagging and dilapidated roof, I could see that there were terrible weeds actually growing out of it for all to see. They had grown ridiculously big. They would have to be rooted out, one by one. Anyone viewing this edifice would not need to see the sag of the roof to know that it was not a protected structure. They would only need to see the size of the weeds coming from it. These weeds were not like Oak trees, however, which would take some work to get down. These weeds were flimsy when the roots were attacked. This was not as big a job as it looked, contrary to the window replacement.

I got the sense that the core of both Churches was intact. If people approached either the Church in disrepair or the Church in its new, heavenly state, they would find Christ but they would certainly have to be brave and sturdy to stay in the dilapidated Church and they would have to be determined to approach if they were newly arrived.

Today I saw the Church again, so beautiful in its purity. I understood that no storm would impact this newly reclaimed Church because it had heavenly stability. I noticed that all of the windows were open, both on the bottom and even in the roof. There was a free flow of graces in and out and such was the force of the "Hosannas" emanating from the inside that the heavenly chorus could be heard all around the world, from this one humble edifice. I sensed strongly that the Source of the power of the prayers and graces was at the core of the inside and I looked inside.

I saw the Eucharist. I became aware of a pulsing, steady, rhythmic beat. I know this beat and I have experienced it many times. I believe it to be the heart of Jesus Christ, which flows steady graces into the place of the divine will. I believe that this humble Church is the source of grace on earth and that the heart of Jesus is what sustains it. I rested in the life-giving beat. My mystical friend asked me how I felt. "Safe," I replied. When one is in this place, listening to this life-giving rhythm, one feels sustained and safe. Regardless of how badly one is suffering, this beat will keep them from perishing. This applies to all of humanity.

I understood the border, the beautiful hedge, to be the holiness of the laity and the clergy, which I can see growing at an enormous rate. This is the renewal. Older borders, or rather parts of borders which have been maintained, will connect with newer movements to merge what is solid about the old to what is life-giving about the new. Both will draw strength from the other and this will create an effect of unity which will be strong because the way the enemy will attack the Church and try to keep it in its dilapidated form will be to keep the old separated from the new. In other words, promote disunity, so that there is no connection which can protect the Church and the area around it. Unity will be an important component of this protective barrier and I see now why Jesus wants our apostolate to work so hard at unifying other holy movements in the Church today. I also saw that the older movements which were faithful had been isolated during this period of disrepair. I could see one fresh-looking one here and there in the midst of others which were dead, dying or trampled.

I want to note that when I saw the dilapidated Church in the dreadful state of disrepair I saw that while many were repulsed from entering, there were still a few doors open with beautiful pathways which had been maintained. These were small and one had to look for them but these openings and pathways continued to draw and people were encouraged to approach the Church but almost did so in the spirit of rebels. There was definitely a feeling of being surreptitious about the ones who came into the Church in its state of dilapidation. They looked as though they feared attack and those drawing them closer were very careful in their shepherding of newly arrived ones.

September 12, 2008

Today my mystical friend showed me that everywhere he looked there was work to be done. I surveyed the Church and surrounding area as he did and I saw what he saw. He is like a tired father looking at all of this, not despairing, but acutely aware of all that needs to be done. I felt a moment's irritation. I said, "How was it allowed to get this bad?" He replied, "Only God knows the full answer to that question. It is not for us to know the details of the crisis. It is enough for us to understand the details of the assignment."

As I watched, I saw many people coming upon the scene. They were each intently involved in some project that was related to the restoration of the Church and surrounding areas. I concentrated on one man in particular who was working to create unity with one of the older groups who had survived the great decline. The older group had what I can describe as a siege mentality and were not open to being connected to the newer movements of the Spirit. This beautiful apostle sat stoically, with great humility and great determination, until the existing 'shrub' received the enlightenment that flowed through him. The older group then became part of the beautiful hedge that will surround the Church. When I noted that the apostle had been successful, I noted that the shrub in that corner joined with another true shrub and became a little protective barrier which would one day unite to the larger finished hedge. I looked around and saw apostles working in this way all over the outside area, uniting, patiently, soothingly creating unity by breaking down barriers. These apostles were willing to be insulted and humiliated in order to bring others together.

I saw two men replacing a window. As I said earlier, this is a treacherous job where blood is drawn because of the embedded nature of the glass that is bad. There is malice attached to this task. The pieces of glass, broken and filthy, do not want to be taken out and as I said it is a piece by piece job. The apostles on this job are humble, like the others, but also extremely selfless. They are willing to be hurt badly, even martyred, for the good of the finished job. I see these apostles as those who are confronting deeply planted enemies of the Church who are actually in the Church. They will be sustained, of course, and will have all that they need. The problem for them is that so often it will appear hopeless and they will feel powerless and then God will step in and the glass will literally fall out into their hands. They will need great trust and faith and through the prayers of others for the Church, they will have these things.

Throughout the area now I could see, with my friend, people working in every area, every corner, cleaning, cutting, gardening, building, consulting with each other. There was great joy and determination and a spirit of service and work that I have seldom observed. The whole site was pure and purity in intention and spirit was noteworthy. I could see a man attempting to create unity and being stung badly. He looked up to see another apostle watching him, empathizing. As they exchanged glances, they began to laugh in commiseration. The sting victim was so relieved that someone else had both observed and understood the attack against him. The other apostle then left his own work to assist the wounded one. The communication exchanged was a moment of intimacy between them. The observer was given the grace to understand exactly how the man charged with diplomacy was struggling and suffering. His loneliness was then gone and the observer left what he was doing for a time and assisted his fellow apostle. In this way, the first apostle was able to maintain his joy in a trying situation. This team spirit was evidenced throughout the scene and it is this spirit of unity that helped the hardworking apostles to retain their joy. I must state that this exchange and consequent assist from one to the other filled me with longing because it was so like heaven. They worked in a fragrance of grace despite their hardships.

September 16, 2008 Monday

Today my mystical friend brought me back to the Church and once again I watched people working. He drew me to a woman in the middle of the front garden. She was working on a fountain. It looked small in size, about four feet tall and somewhat like a wedding cake but not a ridiculously big one. She was doing intricate work and as I watched her, I loved her very much. My mystical friend loved her too and I said, "This is very important to you." He agreed and said, "What would you say to her, Anne?" I studied her again and I studied her project. I could see that she was seriously determined to get one part of it right, let's say the top tier. She had a vision of how the water should flow out equally from one place in four different directions. I could see that this subtlety would impact the whole flow down through each tier. I could see what she was trying to achieve. There was pressure on her from others to give up the idea as it was causing a lot of work for her and them, but she continued to study it and make the smallest adjustments. Her concentration was fierce. I said, "I would protect her right to reflect the true Spirit she has been given for this assignment. I would encourage her to keep working until she gets it the way she wants it. Only she has the purity of this vision and she should be given all that she needs to perfect it, regardless of what others say. She should not be pushed into compromising." My friend was delighted with this answer and agreed. I became curious. I wondered why it was so important to him and asked. He said that this was something he had championed and protected and it meant a lot to him as he shared the vision of this woman. He said, "Once it is right it can be replicated throughout the Church. Until then, it must remain small and she must remain obscure." I promised him that I would pray for this woman and this project and that I would help in any way he asked. It is not a religious order, I do not think. It has something to do with sexuality and women and children or women and how they mother their children. I will know it, I believe, when I see it on earth.

I was then drawn to the back of the Church and up to the top where there was a bell tower. There was something wrong with the bell. It still rang and could be heard, but it had the capability to play extraordinary heavenly music. For a moment, I was allowed to hear it playing in the way that it was supposed to and the way that my friend wanted it to play. It was so glorious as to make one laugh out loud. I had a moment of realization of how those close to me would rejoice in this and wished they could hear it but I know that some day they will. It was a great gift to be allowed to hear the purity of the notes harmonizing in the clear air. It was like heaven to me and I felt a feeling of reassurance that I would one day be there forever. After this moment, I could see even more clearly the disrepair. I saw that there were many bells and that they were intended to play in beautiful harmony but that many did not sound at all and many others emitted discordant and disturbing notes. Some were really off. I was told that each bell represented the Church in a different country. I understood that this project would ultimately give great glory to Our Lady and the project has to do with Our Lady. I said, "This looks like a long term project." He said, "Use the word 'ongoing'." I can see that there will be a lot of people responsible for getting this right because each bell needs to be adjusted in this ongoing way. That stated, there needs to be an immediate renovation undertaken.

I was drawn by my friend out into the front of the Church. He pointed out, away from the Church. I saw people out for miles. Some were fallen-aways, some were non-Catholics. It was dark out there and the people actually looked like they were in a charcoal dark world. They looked a little dirty, actually. The area where we stood was light and clean and I saw that as the world grew darker, people began to turn toward us and make their way to us. I thought, "How in heaven's name will we accommodate them all?"

And there's no stopping them. They are coming. My friend said, "I want those who have arrived working. Do you understand?"

I did. He is saying that if a person has returned to the Church or has never left the Church, that person should be working hard on the renovations in the Church in order to prepare for those who are returning now and those who will return in the future. Everybody needs to be working and concentrating. The Church needs to be sounding the bells and providing a light, clean place so that others can see where they should come for safety. There is something to be known about other Christian Churches but perhaps that will come tomorrow.

September 17, 2008 Tuesday

First I saw the Church as it is today from the perspective of my mystical friend. It is in a state of disrepair and not functioning as God wants it to function. I looked around the front of it and saw the apostles working steadily. Suddenly, I saw them being attacked or persecuted. I looked from one to the next and the notable thing was that this was occurring simultaneously. There were attempts to distract them from their projects; there were loud noises and scary sounds. An apostle would look at something occurring across the yard and have the greatest difficulty in remaining concentrated on his own task. As this occurred, worse in some places than others, I saw apostles coming to each other's assistance, shoring up each project with additional support. As others came to join in the efforts, apostles were better able to keep their focus and keep working. It is very important to state that despite the persecutions, which were considerable, the projects all over the yard moved along. Progress was not delayed. It just meant more suffering and more toughness needed.

My friend said, "What is happening to the apostles, Anne?" I saw them growing in holiness and sturdiness as well as growing in great numbers.

Next I was taken back to the Church building itself, still in the state of disrepair. I noted the huge weeds which were both obstructing the Eucharist on the inside and sticking out through the roof. The apostles working to reclaim the Church in its purity were being attacked by the weeds. In other words, the attacks were coming from a few who appeared to be working inside the Church. I realize what I am writing here and I am only writing it because it is what I saw. I saw a holy man, a Pope, kneeling in front of the Eucharist which was exposed on the altar with candles that made the lighting beautiful and consoling. The Pope was a smart man. He knew that the way to support the apostles outside was to pray for God's power. He was connected to their endeavors and he prayed for their endeavors constantly. His great holiness and unity with the Eucharistic Jesus insured that his prayers were pure and so pleasing to the Father that the Father could only answer them in completeness according to His holy will. I saw that this man, the Pope, was being given great lights of truth and clarity so that his communications exposed the teachings of those who were puffed up as without merit or without true heavenly substance.

At the time of the persecution, there were holy apostles inside the Church, working away at the roots of these big weeds. They appeared so small comparatively in that they did not try to be impressive. They seemed to have humble and child-like spirits of concentration about them as they dug at the base of these weeds with implements that appeared to them to be like kitchen spoons. In other words, they felt out of their league and wondered constantly if they could be effective. They were extremely effective and I could see Our Lady smiling at them and protecting their efforts. They were digging trenches around the base of these weeds, again, the roots of which, when exposed, were in actual fact ridiculously fragile despite the silly height and reach of the weeds. These workers delighted me because of their humility and determination. They must concentrate on the vulnerability of the root and the true fact that the weeds are obstructing the view of the faithful from Jesus Christ. At the appointed time, Jesus will simply extend a heavenly hand and pull the weeds out right through the ceiling. Because of the work of these faithful men and women at the base of these things, the weeds will come out swiftly, easily and completely and I understand that heaven will not allow a recurrence of this situation, meaning this level of obstruction within His Church proper.

After the weeds had been removed, I could see that the bells were liberated. The workers up in the bell tower who were working so hard became completely free to operate in speed and I could hear an instant tuning going on, as well as the beginnings of harmonies in various groups of bells. This was a remarkably joyful occurrence and I must state an awareness that nobody really understood the full restrictive nature of the weeds on these bells until the weeds had been removed. The apostles working around the Church, meaning, out in the world, felt great freedom and ease at this time as well. This was an important purification for the Church.

After all of this, after the weeds were gone and the apostles were working steadily outside and the floors were treated inside the Church and the bells were tuned and repaired, I sensed a hushed and reverent time, a waiting, a great expectation. I was drawn to the inside of the Church and I could see the power of God bursting out in graces through the Eucharist. All were affected. All were blessed. All were confirmed and rewarded in that they felt doubts disappearing and felt their hearts opened far more completely to heaven's presence in the Eucharist and in their individual hearts. There were magnificent healings happening during this period, and this is a period rather than a moment. It will continue. What is the difference between this time and the time before? Apostles are still working but they are working in a Church and surrounding area that is clean and filled with light and clarity. There is terrific fellowship and love between them with very little territorial sparring. Holy apostles do not spar, by the way, they defend, however they can be tempted and I saw that the temptations to do this in this New Time were minimal. There was unity in service and growth in holiness. It was still earthly existence but it was earthly existence in a Church that had been cleaned, refreshed and renewed.

September 18, 2008 Wednesday

Today I watched apostles working in the area in front of the Church. My eyes were drawn outside of that circle, to the area outside of the Church and its environs. I could see the people out in the world again and I noted in particular those who looked in on the Church from the immediate area around it. I saw painful longing in their eyes. They so badly wanted to be in the area of light. I could see that many of them felt they could not possibly fit in or be accepted. Some, because of this feeling of rejection, which was founded in some cases and unfounded in others, lashed out at the Church. In their pain they began to tear the Church down, throwing rocks or what have you. It actually became groups of people in some areas where, lets say they saw a broken window and began to all throw rocks at it in an ugly sporting like way to destroy the window even further. We kind of have this coming, (I add editorially), as what they are identifying as hypocrisy, is, in some cases, hypocrisy. This does not excuse hooliganism, but in some cases it can explain it.

At any rate, protecting filthy broken windows had nothing to do with me and would not serve the Church and I felt my attention drawn back to the outside perimeter. I knew that some of these people were keeping themselves out. They had no reason to believe that they would not be welcomed. They had to make a decision to step into this light and then begin helping. There is something extraordinary about the immediate area outside of the Church perimeter. I am really fascinated here at this area as I have felt frustrated that there was not an ante-room or porch or receiving area for fallen-aways where they could come and examine the Church's true teachings in light of their false beliefs and then be assisted back into the sacramental life of the Church in any way possible. Something has to be done, truly, in God's name people have to be more effectively welcomed back. I do not say change the standards but we have to do better at making them welcome.

Back to the vision, I saw far out into the world, and I saw lights which I immediately recognized as apostles. They were out in the world pointing and directing people back to the safety of the Church. I saw them being pushed and jostled but they kept working. I saw one man who had organized and a stream of about twenty across marched steadily back into the Church. He was really effective and that was his job, which he had said yes to, and God was using him to the fullest in his humility. I thought of two men I know working in the world doing this. I next saw a woman working in the world. She was in the crowd and she would get one person, who would then hold onto her hand. She would pull this person back to the Church with the greatest determination, pulling the person through distracting crowds and knots of people and eventually and always, delivering the person back to the Church yard where she would push them in and then go back and get the next person Jesus identified as her project. She was a point guard person. The others were zone people, to use basketball terms. She was as important as the ones who brought groups of people and one of the men in charge of bringing the groups had been brought back to the Church by this woman. This makes it so clear to me how important our humble daily service is to heaven, even though we do not see it that way. This glimpse of those working in the world delighted me.

My mystical friend asked me, "You see their lights shining in the world, Anne. Where do they get this light?"

I saw that their light was coming from the Eucharist in the heart of the Church building. I saw that it was the exact same light as the light that radiated out from the Eucharist that the Holy Father knelt before in Adoration. I saw that for this light to remain bright in the world, the apostles had to come back to the origin, the Eucharist, regularly. They are linked with heaven's will this way. If they do not continue to receive the graces from the Eucharist, the light in them becomes dimmer and dimmer. This is bad because they then become vulnerable and God's plan in them also becomes vulnerable.

September 18, 2008 Thursday

Today I looked out again into the world where many had fallen away. I saw the lights from the apostles and as I watched, more and more lights began to be apparent. I thought to myself, "This must be the renewal." One of the effects of this was that it became more and more difficult for fallen-aways to deny their condition. Each time they faced an apostle who authentically possessed Christ, in other words, one who was not part of the ring of defiance, they were compelled to notice the reality of their own condition. Being in the presence of those who possessed this light had the effect of forcing them to look in the mirror, so to speak. Another effect of these increased numbers of apostles in the world was to give greater courage to those serving. In some areas, as I watched, one light shone brightly, then, suddenly, around that person many, many lights began to be seen. I saw this again and again in different places. Truly, it makes me think that the Spirit is doing marvelous and miraculous things in this time.

September 18, 2008 Friday

Today my mystical friend brought me back to the front of the Church where I watched the woman adjusting her fountain. She was doing delicate work, adjusting the four pieces of marble that would direct the flow of the water in four directions. I sensed again the importance of the work for the future and I sensed my mystical friend's interest and hope in this project. Next, I looked out beyond this scene further out into the 'yard' and saw that the light was changing. I looked up to see the sky darkening. Everyone continued working, I noticed, which was the point. The apostles could see that the sky was darkening, but they continued to concentrate on the tasks that they were assigned. This was how the mystical friend wanted them to work. He approved of the way they did not allow the distraction of the darkening sky to throw them off task. I saw that in some areas, a whirlwind would descend on a project and group and it would be like a tornado in that all that they had erected was torn down and destroyed. This was a stunning blow for those involved and I saw that it was terribly important that those unaffected provide support for the victims of these storms. I saw an apostle drawing one such affected apostle away from the debris and assigning him to another task to give him time to heal and take it in. This was a good strategy for recovery. I saw a large area which was attached to the outer perimeter on one side. It was vast and it was barren. I looked into the Church and saw that the Holy Father was praying especially for this area. He was asking God to alert apostles to go there and support the Catholics there who, from what I was shown, are struggling with very little assistance from the outside, where, comparatively, there is great richness in the Church. I saw that the Holy Father understood the connection between some of the edifices being erected in the garden and the future assistance to this barren land. I understood that the fountain of the woman would send a stream of life-giving waters in that direction which would pierce the boundary of this barren place and flow into it under the ground. I saw the barren land and I saw that across it, where there were lights, this stream of water appeared from underneath and began to seep into the areas where it came up to the surface. I saw the lights then multiplying, both from the local areas and from apostles going into the barren area from outside of it. This was good. When the storms landed on groups working, I could see that the storms scoured the areas. It was violent. But I also saw that the imprint of the work remained in the air, like structures of light that could not be destroyed, only temporarily obscured by an obstacle. I am trying to say that the storms could not destroy what the apostles had created. The imprint of their work remained permanently in an area to be later reclaimed and filled out again, sometimes by others coming later. The imprint then provided a blueprint for other holy apostles, even though they were often unaware of it. This was beautiful and joyful and showed me again how the communion of saints works. Nobody should ever think that the work they have done for God either in buildings that are concrete or in buildings that are mystical, can be destroyed. These holy works are eternal in nature and as such invulnerable.

Later, I again noted the darkening sky. As noted before, the apostles continued working. I saw rain begin to pelt them from the sky. I said, "They're going to get wet. Why aren't they seeking shelter?" My mystical friend replied, "They're not afraid to get wet, Anne." I wondered about lightning, thinking of the storms of my childhood, which were dangerous. "They're not afraid," he repeated. "Why aren't they afraid, Anne?" I looked at them and saw that the Eucharistic Christ was present in their souls, in other words, the same light that comes from the altar where the Eucharist is exposed for Adoration. Because they knew Christ was within them, they trusted the Father to care for them.

"What if their projects get damaged or destroyed?" I asked. "They will repair or rebuild them," he answered. I understood this but the humanity in me still wondered if they should not seek shelter. Then I realized something. Where could they go? Nowhere. They could not leave the Church. That was not an option for them as it would not be option for me. I would have to say that it would be better for me to die in place than abandon the work the Lord has willed for me. They must be thinking the same way, much like the apostle, Peter.

I saw that the dark skies were moving past. This is notable. Even if dark skies appear to be stalled over an area, they are not stalled. They are passing all the time. I saw the area of light coming. Most of the Church remained under the cloud but suddenly the light hit the bell tower and the warmth from the sun triggered the bells ringing. They rang in harmony and all of them were working perfectly. I could see Our Lady presiding over this and knew that it was her influence and prayer that enabled them to begin ringing and to have been put in such a state of order and function. As Our Lady watched, the sun moved gradually over the rest of the Church and area and there was relief and joy for the apostles. I saw Our Lady presiding over all of this as her Son, from inside the Church on the altar, flowed divine graces out into every apostle.

I will say that when I saw the grace flow seeping from under the ground into the barren area, Our Lady was standing above the whole thing. It was when she raised her eyes to the Father in supplication that I saw the stream of grace being drawn under the ground to the places where it emerged like a fresh water spring. Our Lady is asking for this grace for the barren land and the Father is answering her prayers. Above ground a battle is being waged that is fierce and very ugly, really ugly but Our Lady's gaze at the Father remains steady and the graces continue to be drawn out into the land. Our Lady is not afraid at all. 'Determined' would be a good way to describe her. Seeing this about her gives me great strength and courage because I can see that this is how it is done. Eyes on the Father, let the storm rage around you and trust in the ultimate triumph of goodness over evil. The prayers affect how it will be done and how quickly it will be accomplished but Our Lady, and by extension all of us, will win in the end.

Unity

"Form yourselves one and all into a choir, that blending in concord and taking the keynote of God, you may sing in unison with one voice through Jesus Christ to the Father that he may hear you and recognize you through your good deeds to be members of His Son. Therefore it is profitable for you to live in blameless unity, that you may always enjoy communion with God"

St. Ignatius to the Ephesians in the year 107

Unity

There is a misconception about unity. People fear that in order to be unified, they will have to abandon truth or abandon the holy positions they hold either in their hearts or in their work. Neither of these beliefs is accurate. Unity requires a disposition of the heart which refuses to condemn. Condemning people is different than making a judgment call on that which is objectively wrong.

It is often not enough for us to follow the path that the Lord has marked out for us. We tend to also examine the paths of others and rather than seeing other paths as authentically belonging to others, we see them as flawed because they do not perfectly match our own. While this is obviously wrong, perhaps it is not always malicious. Perhaps it is part of the limitation of our humanity and consequent short-sightedness.

That stated, we are all asked to extend ourselves beyond our humanity and I believe that in order for the renewal to advance, we must all make a heroic effort to acknowledge in our hearts and words and actions, that if we desire unity, will have to adjust the way we view others.

October 31, 2008

In order to promote unity for all Christians, we, Catholics must acquire it ourselves. If we actively seek complete unity in our Church, we will, at the very least, make gains and acquire greater unity tomorrow than we have today. When we do this, we will not only be setting an example of heavenly fraternity for other faiths, we will be providing the world with a secure love source wherein people can find mystical shelter. There is nothing worse than entering a household where there is tension, after all, and those households are not attractive to either visitors or those seeking guidance. Visitors are too distracted by the tension to benefit. But consider those households where there is harmony and love, not perfectly, of course, but generally. People are drawn to these households because they find good example, emotional safety and a resting spot. Weary searchers battered by disunity in their own faiths can be strengthened enough to continue.

We might say that our destiny as a Church is to be a stronghold of love for the Father but we can only fulfill our destiny as a Church if we allow God to bring us to greater unity.

Unity can happen very quickly if there is a push for humility. You see, dear apostles, it is arrogance that thwarts unity. "I am right" is not the correct disposition for a unity campaign. "We all love God and we are all trying hard to serve Him," is a better disposition. We see so much squabbling and positioning. We see so much judgment and superiority. We cannot simply point fingers out in this area. We must always point our fingers at ourselves first and identify those areas where we are judgmental. Yes, there is work for us all in the area of humility and unity.

Catholics, even some holy Catholics, do not follow the rightful authorities in the Church. This is of grave concern. Instead, they follow notions which have taken root in their hearts and from which the enemy proceeds out with superiority and judgment. If the rightful authority gives guidance and consent on a matter, then who has the right to be disparaging of this position? I would not like to be the one arguing with Jesus Christ about why I knew better about matters of unity in His Church than the authorities. This should make every Catholic pause and consider. We are often pulling against the Kingdom when we do this. If we pray for the authority in question and attempt a respectful dialogue, then often we will find unity in time.

In examining our Church, it is clear that the body has many parts, all important, all necessary. Given that the body has many parts, it is vulnerable to breakdown in terms of the humanity present in God's plan. We accept this and yet we work tirelessly against such breakdown because we do not want anything to interrupt the forward motion of the Body of Christ.

I recently viewed a situation where there is not only disunity in the

Church, but great confusion and misunderstanding. I wondered, 'Who is the rightful arbitrator of truth?' As a Catholic, it is evident to me that God's plan includes His Pontiff leading as the rightful arbitrator of His truth in the Church. If not the Holy Father, then whom? Which Catholic man or woman would hold himself or herself above the Holy Father as the rightful arbitrator of truth? Who would push their body in front of his and pretend to have greater wisdom? Who would listen to the Holy Father speak the truth and then try to drown out his voice with his own version of the truth?

It is true that sometimes when Truth is offered it bumps into self-will and arrogance, is subverted and what is light becomes dimmer or darker or less audible. The truth will remain, of course, as it cannot change, however it is less likely to be recognized. The faithful are distracted by voices speaking simply to be heard.

If the Holy Father is the rightful arbitrator of truth in certain matters, then where is the benefit to God's plan for humanity in pulling against him? He is merely one who executes, after all. It is God we are pulling against. Will God allow negative consequences to come from a pure spirit of humility which seeks to uphold the rightful authority in the Church? How could He? This would mean that Jesus would be exchanging bad will for good will. This would be impossible. I am saying that there is no compelling circumstance where we would be making a mistake by supporting the Pope.

People drowning out the voice of the Holy Father through rebellion and disagreement are pulling against God Himself.

How can we advance without the power of unity? It cannot be done. Consider a herd of cattle and the effort to move them to another place. A unified forward momentum is necessary and all efforts at advancing the herd go to this objective, which is, keeping the cattle moving in the same direction.

God wills renewal. We are charged with participating in this renewal. In order to do our part we must make sure that we fall in behind the Holy Father in a spirit of humility and unity.

There will always be those claiming to be savvier than the Holy Father, or better informed, or more sophisticated. Often they do not say this outright but imply it with subtle reproaches that signal arrogance and superiority. It can be difficult to sift through these things when those who rebel possess great learning. Those of us lacking such study can find ourselves intimidated. But we should not be. We should feel confident in the leadership of our Pontiff and offer our simplicity and lack of sophistication to the Lord, who will honor our fidelity with dignity and holiness. When someone claims to be more 'in the know' than our Pope, we must be very alert indeed.

There are those who will argue, "He is just a man and he does not always lay claim to infallibility." To this I would respond "True. He, himself would say the same, but he is the only person chosen to lead as Pope at this time." He is certainly more chosen than I am to lead the Church and this statement applies to every other person on earth.

The question that must be asked is this. Do we desire our will or God's will? If we truly desire God's will, that is, worldwide renewal, then we must resist all temptation to arrogance. God has given us a leader worthy of the title. This leader now requires many others to rise up and face the same way, echoing his call to unity.

What I have observed is alarming in this way. There are those who are chosen to also lead in the Church, but whose call is, of course, to lead by following the Pontiff. But they do not want to follow. They want to build houses on their personal opinions, which cannot be more ordained by heaven than the Holy Father's opinions. Many see that these people do not want unity. They want to be right. They want to be justified. This craving to be justified does not come from God. Which man is justified on earth? None of us should desire this. We should be content to be justified by God in heaven. What is the poor Holy Father to do with us? He shares God's love for us all. He wants us to be confirmed in grace. If there is too much self-love, there is no room for God's unifying love.

Tuesday

When praying about unity, my mind rested on the image of a racing boat in a competition. The athletes worked together in a way that seemed perfect. I watched in breathless admiration as their boat sliced through the water at great speed. Each athlete seemed perfectly concentrated on being part of the team and using all of his physical skills and mental concentration on advancing the project, which was to move the boat forward at the greatest possible speed. This image was powerful and brought to mind the call to unity in our Church.

We must all be like those athletes. They were not positioning themselves, one over the other. They were not bickering over whose position was bringing the most benefit to the boat in particular or to the race in general. They were not hitting each other over the heads with their oars. Rather, they were using all that God had given them to work together on the same cause. Each benefitted individually by becoming, through committed service on the team, the best possible athlete he or she could become. There was joy and invigoration.

When we work in unity with other Catholics, both in our hearts and in our words and actions, we are like the team members in this boat who speed their craft forward with no impediment. The possibility for the advancement of the renewal in this time is thrilling. The more we come together, the quicker this will happen.

Monday November 10, 2008

On the other side as a possibility is that we will not move toward unity, but further away from unity. In that case, while Jesus never wills a schism, He will allow one. He will have no choice. He will have to act protectively for the preservation of the purity of the Church. The ramifications of this would be very sad for all of humanity because the strength and vigor of the Church impacts all humanity. In the case of a schism, is it possible that God's authority will move with the break-away faction? No. It is not possible but He is so merciful that He will not abandon those in error.

God's authority and power and revelatory graces will remain with the Chair of Peter. He will be present there, even until the end of time.

Is this idea of schism a real threat? Well, I think it is. I think what we are experiencing in the past period may be many small schisms. We can think of them like small tears in the fabric of a cloak. If there are enough tears, and these tears join, we will get big tears that actually separate a piece of the cloth from the cloak. What remains? A smaller cloak which is less capable of effectively fulfilling its function which is to warm a body, in this case, the Body of Christ. Men of good will can only control this in as much as they defend God's truth in our faith and in as much as they do so in a spirit of humility, love and conciliation. Men of good will can only control this in as much as they seek to move to unity with the Holy Father in any and all areas where they are tempted to disunity.

How would I handle a situation where I am tempted to disunity to our Holy Father? I have experienced this in my life and I simply had to eventually conclude that I did not fully understand the teaching. I sought understanding and eventually Jesus delivered it to both my head and my heart.

I was certain of a couple of truths at that time. One, I was not the Pope. Two, it was probable that I lacked the full picture. I surmised that if someone had to move, it was most likely me.

If we can all accept that we do not know everything, we will be a good starting point for unity.

November 11, 2008

There are those who will say that disunity or schism is always a threat in our Church. They are correct and we have seen these things occur in the past. However, we will not be accountable for anything that occurred on someone else's watch. We will be accountable for what occurred on our watch if we fail to follow God's will for us and stand up when we should.

We must accept that schism is never the Lord's plan. It is the enemy's plan. We must accept that schism is the enemy's goal, his priority in destroying the greatest receptacle of God's truth on earth, that is, the Catholic Church. If we correctly view schism as our enemy's constant goal, we must also view it as a constant threat and a constant area where we do maintenance work on ourselves, our organizations and our relationships with other holy organizations. We have to continually shore up our defenses.

We always return to the need for humility. Will the reader throw this writing down because I repeat myself and talk of humility incessantly? People fly past the word, acknowledging its importance but we must stop at the word and examine ourselves.

Organizations who do not root out pride and arrogance will not flourish. They will gradually die out in terms of their effectiveness in spreading the Gospel message of love. To be clear, they may be very successful as worldly endeavors but they will house less of the Spirit and over time lose their vibrancy.

What does God do about this? He inspires newer organizations to take their place. Someone recently told me that Ireland had no need for religious orders because the government now provided for the charitable needs of the people. Such nonsense. Of course we need religious orders but we need humble religious orders who remember the One they serve and who fulfill the call to be servants. Religious orders are always necessary to serve God and

His children.

It is clear that all Catholic organizations must flow upward to and through the Chair of Peter. I can see that authentic graces flow downward from heaven through this Chair and into our human activities taken on in the name of our faith. As such, we must have exquisite respect for all who serve in the same manner.

I believe that Jesus suffers grief over organizations who cite strict adherence to the Church and yet who, in spirit, detract from the authority of the Church by superiority to the Pope. "He's getting it wrong," is not the refrain of a person who is obedient in action and spirit. People so often forget that the Holy Father has children all across the globe, not just in any one region or country. As such he is responsible for parenting a diverse family.

An example is when the Holy Father speaks of a specific problem such as world hunger and others erupt as though the Holy Father had rebuked the importance of the issue they were chosen to combat. Stating the truth about world hunger in no way detracts from the peril of other pressings problems which threaten God's children. This may be comparable to a sibling becoming petulant and pouty when a human father pays much needed attention to a younger brother. Love for one does not necessarily equal neglect of the other.

I believe that there are many Catholic organizations who might try to aim more directly for the Chair of Peter. Heaven's graces can then become more fully available to them. All authentic representations of Jesus Christ have a hallmark of drawing in as much as God desires growth. The Trinity is invitational, after all. Organizations united to the Trinity are also invitational. The word invitational brings to mind gentle beckoning. The word invitational does not bring to mind judgment or superiority. Jesus was neither of these things. Jesus listened to people. Jesus saw things from the perspective of the person in front of Him, regardless of the judgments of others on that person.

To repeat the salient point in another way, each Catholic individual and each Catholic organization must examine himself or his organization to determine whether or not his efforts flow upward through the Chair of Peter to heaven. If there is a miss, then he or his organization must move or adjust their aim because one thing is for certain. Jesus Christ is not going to move the Chair.

If we think we will die and go to heaven and tell Jesus that we directed our Catholic personal life or our Catholic organization's efforts up to heaven but not through the Chair of Peter, we will have to explain it. Now maybe we think Jesus will say, "You did well to protect your life or organization from the leadership I willed in My Church". But I suspect it is more likely He will say, "You were confused, My friend". He might even say, "You were prideful". I do not know. I have no way of knowing what will happen but I urge everyone to consider that since the Chair is not likely to move for our opinions, we had better adjust our courses where they need adjusting and line up to aim for the Chair.

Sometimes, unity costs us something and there are many things we can offer for unity. We can offer our pride for unity. We can offer our opinions as long as we do not compromise with what we know to be true and right. We can offer pain that is inflicted on us by others. These things can be given to Jesus, our pride, our opinions and our pain, for the sake of unity in His Church. I in no way suggest that we compromise with the truth or with the true teachings of the Church that come from rightful Church authority. Rather, I am saying that we should not march into battle to fight our friends and allies.

From the Epistle of Jude we read...But Michael the archangel when he disputed with the devil and argued about the body of Moses, did not dare pronounce against him a railing judgment but said, "The Lord rebuke you". (Jude 1:9)

St. Michael did not dare pronounce a judgment against Satan and yet sometimes we hand judgment down as though it were our personal right. This does not come from holy men but from those who think they are holy, those who clean their front yards but not their houses or their back yards. In other words, it looks like a good cow but it is producing bad milk that does not nourish others but sickens them over time. Others are drawn into the darkness of passing judgment. If we busy ourselves passing judgment, my friends, we have been distracted by the enemy and cunningly drawn into his campaign of spreading darkness. How effectively he uses us against our brothers and sisters who long for Christ and who long for reunion with the family of God. Really, I think Satan must enjoy such delight at using those who are called to preach the Gospel against that very Gospel message.

Michael understood that only God could pronounce judgment and that judgment was God's right. The idea that mankind has anywhere near what he needs to make a correct judgment against a man's heart is the greatest pride, although it comes from pride. It is evidence of man being brought by Satan to his most ridiculous through pride. It is also very sad because in many of these cases man has become so deluded that he is persuaded that he pronounces judgment against one man to lead others to safety when in fact he does the opposite. Better we pray for those we suspect are evil than we make sweeping and definitive judgments against them in the foolishness of our pride.

This is a good time to remind ourselves that based on the darkness in each one of us anyone could pronounce judgment against us. What if they did it publicly as many are doing today? Would this be fair or accurate?

St. Michael understood that he was not God. So should we.

Thursday November 20, 2008

In this time, the world is filled with critics. Everyone knows better. Everyone has an opinion. This is fine if one is conducting oneself in truth and one limits his opinions to his own work or to those who seek out an opinion from him about their work. This is not always the case, however.

It seems there is a general tearing down with little awareness of what one is tearing down. We are tearing down each other.

The world is not made up entirely of Catholics but the fact that others do not agree with us about our faith does not give us permission to behave badly toward them. It is most certainly a shame that others treat us badly. We have biblical evidence, though, of how the followers of Christ are treated so we are consoled and strengthened when we remind ourselves that our persecutions, both small and large, are fully within apostolic tradition.

To focus our beam of light within the Church, we can see that there are many authentic movements of the Spirit. We repeat this because it is a cause for joy for all holy apostles. God needs unity between these movements. And yet, we do not have anything near unity. Catholics can cause each other the greatest pain and suffering by assaulting other Catholics.

In this time, Jesus Christ is asking for a serious movement toward unity. To obtain this, all apostles must rise each day and renew their commitment to unity in the Church. Each day, we must ask ourselves where Jesus Christ is going to use us for this goal. We must be alert to His project. Maybe it is in our family, our faith community or in our secular community. Maybe it is in our order, our parish or in our work community. And maybe, it is simply our own heart that unity is lacking.

Poor humanity. The enemy tempts us so relentlessly. We are so often brought to understand that there are those with enmity against us. The enemy tries to persuade us that others are a threat to us. This distracts us and puts us in a defensive posture in our heart. We can never relax and serve in joy if we are always preparing for the next attack. The attacks that do come are inflated by the enemy of peace and he draws us as far as he can into each distraction. And these are distractions.

Perhaps we must ask ourselves what it is that we can do about those who are truly our enemies. Most of the time, we are simply called to pray. Some of the time, we are called to respond in truth with love and gentleness. All of the time we are called to be disciplined about God's work, the work that He wills for us. We have to prevent ourselves from being distracted by those who have decided that it is their holy call to tear down rather than to build up. We have to discern God's call for us and then work, steadily and constantly, trusting the Lord to protect His interests in our souls and in the service that emanates from our souls. If we do this, the Lord can look after Himself in terms of His goals.

I am at a loss to communicate the seriousness of the Lord's call to unity. I am fearful that some of those who believe themselves to be God's closest followers are in fact those who are creating the biggest distractions and drawing others into uncertainty and disunity. Let each man examine himself and let him make a commitment today not to speak in opposition to the Church authority unless Jesus Christ wills that words come from his mouth or pen.

If the world is facing a difficult time, and it seems that we are, then we will need to work very hard to understand God's power and stop talking about darkness. Is the darkness there? Of course. Only a spiritually blind man would deny this. But we sometimes add to the darkness instead of holding up the light. We can be guilty of doing this by talking incessantly of the darkness with dire threats of impending doom. In most cases, we are speculating. Perhaps we should speculate on how God can rescue us and posit those theories instead of hypothesizing how the enemy will play with us next. Perhaps we will speculate on how the Church will lead us with strength and courage instead of how we will be overcome. Perhaps we could try an exercise and guess how good men will become great men through challenges instead of guessing how men of apparent lesser good will become evil through temptation.

May the Lord have mercy on us for being so pessimistic about God's world and may the Lord enlighten us as to how we bring unity to God's Church and not division.

If we identify that unity is desirable, and indeed necessary for the advancement of the renewal, then we will make a decision to participate in the acquisition of this unity. Jesus loves us so much. He has such tremendous hope placed in each one of us and in each one of the roles we have been assigned. Buried in each one of our roles is a portion of work that is marked 'Unity'. We each have a certain amount of responsibility for unity in the Church. It may be a big portion, as in the Holy Father's, or it may be a smaller portion, as in a Catholic serving on a Parish Council, or it may be something that appears even smaller, as in a parishioner who refuses to criticize a parish priest.

Built into each one of these roles is responsibility for unity in the world, among God's children. This may be as big as a leader of state or it may be as less obvious as the children of a family who are called to promote unity in their home or in their school or in the groups within their community. Certainly, at the very least, or perhaps I should say at the very most, we are all part of an earthly family and we are all called to promote unity in our family.

Unity is not a thing that always appears instantaneously probable or even possible. That makes no difference. It is the same as chastity or any virtue in that there are times when the acquisition of such a thing seems impossible. But nothing is impossible with God's grace and unity is not only possible, it is God's plan and therefore must become part of our plan.

I can hear many apostles saying, "These others do not want unity. They refuse to work for unity. Unity is not possible and it is not desirable because these others are getting it wrong."

Well, this would be a predictable and understandable position. We have all experienced situations where those we seem called to work with appear to be impossible to work with. And it is possible that they will outright reject God's call to unity. Let this be if it is to be but we must be alert to the temptation to participate negatively in the situation. We, as apostles, must be blameless.

Yes, we are all called to be as blameless as possible in the temptations to disunity that swirl through the Church today.

How can we be blameless? How can we please Jesus in this regard? ˙ There are a few ways.

One, we must be willing to absorb some degree of hurt for unity. Jesus absorbed the crucifixion in His body and soul in order to protect us. We must be willing to absorb a little bit of humiliation and hurt for Him.

I remember once thinking back on a conversation with a fellow lay apostle. I was concerned that something I said might have been misconstrued and might have caused unintentional hurt. I prayed and Jesus showed me this individual's heart. It was big and open and filled with love. He said, "Do not worry. This heart is so filled with love it can easily absorb a little dart of pain for Me."

I could see that my statement had indeed been misconstrued but that the apostle had taken this in God's light with no ill effect. Even as I resolved to clarify the situation, I rejoiced because I could see that this person was willing to accept far more than an unintended statement and persevere in the work that God willed for us. If only we were all as filled with love and as willing to accept little hurts in humility.

Another way we can please Jesus in the need for unity is to work constantly at seeing situations from the perspective of the other. We may be quite certain that another person is in error. If this is the case, we must study how that person came to be in error. Is it through past hurt? Through a flawed representation of God's truth by people around him? Is it through fear? Through insecurity? Emotional instability?

Distorted thinking can come from many sources and we need to consider that it may not be our job to disabuse another person or organization of a faulty position. There are many times, with God's grace, when we will see that it is most certainly not our call to do so. More likely, it is our call to listen with compassion and commiserate with the crosses of those around us and lead through our example. Also, we usually are not privileged to have all of the information about another so our judgments are based in incomplete information and thus inaccurate. How dangerous we can be to the cause of unity.

Of course we will not be influenced into giving way on God's truths, but neither should we make it our personal quest to straighten everyone out. If we remember this, Jesus will be pleased.

In other words, we must identify the work that God wills for a relationship. We must then try hard to deliver that work to heaven. We want to meet God's goals and be at peace in the flaws of those around us. With God's grace and holy charity, others will be at peace in our flaws. There will never be one person or one group who gets everything right. We should not take this personally. Most are getting a lot of things right so we should try hard to concentrate on what those around us are accomplishing for the Kingdom.

A third way we could please Jesus in this regard is to support the rightful authorities in God's Church. Remember that in the harsh light of Satan, everyone looks suspect. With the smallest bit of information, each one of us could be condemned. If a priest is getting something wrong, no doubt ten people will jump up to tell him. If a bishop is getting something wrong, no doubt one hundred people will jump up to tell him. Unless God absolutely insists, let us not be one of those. Let us, instead, build up our priests and bishops. Let us, as lay apostles, be the person who surrounds our priests with support. When I hear people criticizing the Holy Father, I am amazed. They will be so embarrassed at their arrogance later when they face Jesus.

The world is always changing and it is certainly changing now. I recently looked at the rhetoric. Some was frightening. I then looked to see what the Church was saying. The authorities in the area of the Church involved spoke with clarity. They spoke with love. The leadership coming from the rightful authorities in the Church was calming, truthful and gave no ground in terms of God's truths. I rejoiced and I know that heaven was pleased. But nobody seemed to listen. The beautiful writings coming from God's shepherds were not shot from computer to computer like so many scare darts. The writings from the Cardinals and Bishops were not shared with joy or discussed over coffee. I felt sad because Jesus does not want people frightened, but reassured. Jesus does not want people drawn into hatred and anger, but into love and understanding. We need to do better here and look to the people charged with leadership in the Church. When we see positive leadership, we must spread these words and not the words of those who are themselves confused and frightened.

Tuesday November 25, 2008

As Christians, we are called to be a community people. Nowhere is this more important than in our work in the Church. If there are many authentic movements in the Church, and we all stipulate to the fact that there are, then we are called to work in unity of spirit with them all. This means that we accept that we are one person or group amongst many. We accept that we all offer something of value to the coming of God's Kingdom. We are reverent in the face of the gifts brought to the effort by our brothers and sisters in other movements. We rejoice in the call to unity even though it requires effort.

Consider the concept tangibly. God gives us a pre-determined project, like a set of toy blocks that He wants us to assemble to make an end product, let's say a castle. Each relationship, either between two people or two organizations, has been given a small castle to construct. Each of these, when placed with others, makes up God's kingdom on earth at this time. We must be serious about the individual projects and their importance in the greater project. We should not consider the apparent size of the project when we assign its value. Only God can assess the value for tomorrow of what we are working on today. Many of us can look at what appeared to be unimportant relationships a few years ago and marvel today at the scope of the plan that God placed between two people. Had the relationships not worked out, the project would not have been possible. Jesus knows the end result of each project. We do not. Only by striving for unity can we get to see the end product of God's plan.

We will not even consider the missed opportunities of the past, which is where those kinds of thoughts can go. Instead, we will consider God's mercy and His creativity at helping get around our humanity. We will focus on God's plan for unity today.

Never underestimate what God can do with our willingness to work at relationships.

We must remain alert to opportunities to help other Christians with their tasks. We must try to be like Jesus in our relationships in that when others hurt us, we will strive for a short memory. When others love us, we will strive never to forget. We are all indebted to many and we must remember to thank God for the help we have been given and trust the Lord to reward those who have helped us. In the Christian walk, there is often no way to repay those who have helped us. God Himself does the rewarding. But we can offer our love and loyalty to our friends while we serve on earth. This is pleasing to God and insures joy during our time of service.

Often we have heard that there is an easy way and a hard way. The easy way is God's way. The hard way is our way. We can do God's work the easy way or we can do God's work the hard way. If we work in unity with our brothers and sisters in the Church, we are doing it the easy way and fraternal joy will be ours. If we do God's work the hard way, isolated, suspicious and condemning, God's joy will flee from the sight of us because it knows it is not welcome.

Joy finds no home in those who fail to seek unity with other serving Christians.

Joy always finds a home in those who seek unity with other serving Christians.

Snapshots of Reality

The Dilemma

"I'd rather go to the dentist," Father Phillip said to his friend. "Why do they do this?"

"Who? Who is doing what?"

Father Phillip sighed deeply and considered his friend, also a priest.

"Why do people ask us to come and bless their homes when they are not married? I mean, what are we supposed to do with that?"

Father Jerry opened his mouth to speak but his friend continued

"It feels like a trap. I bless the house and say nothing, I'm colluding. I refuse to bless the house, I'm rejecting. If I state the obvious, they'll say it's none of my business. That happened to me, you know. I asked a couple planning a baptism for their child if they'd ever considered getting married and they got furious. They told me it was none of my business."

Father Jerry nodded sympathetically. "You have to go out to them."

"I know," Father Phillip responded. "But I cannot go and say nothing."

"Of course not. What will you say?"

"I'll ask them if they want a Catholic blessing or a government blessing."

Father Jerry looked at his friend reproachfully.

"Okay," Father Phillip amended, "Maybe that's not the most loving approach. I'll have to give it some thought."

Pulling into the driveway of the young couple's home that evening, Father Phillip offered the last of many prayers. The similar situation he referred to had gone very badly and he was determined that this time be better.

"Give me the words," he prayed.

"We are just about finished with the decorating," the young woman said. She, Mathilde, and her partner, Larry looked to be in their late twenties. "It is certainly a lot of work." She exchanged looks with Larry, a handsome man who looked confident and successful.

"The house is beautiful," Father Phillip acknowledged warmly. "I can see how much care you have put into it."

"Let me show you around," Larry offered.

They walked from room to room, discussing the features of the house. Father Phillip admired the intricacies and noted the loving attention to detail. They entered a room delegated to become an office. For now it remained empty except for a large fish tank which sat on a table at one end of the room. Father Phillip owned a similar one and had always kept fish.

"That's a beautiful tank," he said sincerely. "Have you had it long?"

The couple groaned and started to laugh. "We inherited it," Mathilde said. "My brother had to leave the country for work and basically left it on our porch. Two of the fish have died already."

Father Phillip walked over to the tank and saw, to his alarm that it badly needed cleaning.

"It might need to be cleaned," Larry observed, stating the obvious. "We don't know a lot about fish but I'm determined to find out how to clean it and get it done this weekend."

"My brother's fish are like his babies," Mathilde said uneasily.

Father Phillip faced Mathilde and Larry after examining it. "You know, it could do with a cleaning all right. I know a little about fish. I have an aquarium like this. Let's do it now."

"We couldn't ask you," Larry said immediately.

"Really," Father Phillip said. "It would be my pleasure. I love this kind of thing. It won't take us a minute." He began rolling up his sleeves and the project began. Over the course of the next hour, an easy camaraderie developed between them. By the end of the job, a comfortable conversation ebbed and flowed.

"Father, you might think we are a bit strange asking you to bless the house and not being married," Mathilde said as they poured water into the kitchen sink. Father Phillip said nothing. "It's just that we want to get married but we don't have the money."

"Do you want a big wedding?" Father Phillip asked.

Larry blew his breath out. "If we even start to talk about a wedding, fights begin. My mother wants one thing and Mathilde's mother wants something else. We can't afford either one of the plans and it seemed like the best thing to do to avoid it until we have more money."

Father Phillip recognized the moment and spoke casually. "You know, I prayed before I came. I asked Jesus what He would want me to say to you. And this is what I believe He would tell you. Jesus loves you both. He is with you in this house and in this relationship. He has blessed you with each other and He wants the best for you. I can see how committed you are to each other. You've taken such loving care with every detail of the house. Maybe getting married would be like taking the same care with your relationship. But I can see your dilemma, of course. Did you ever consider going away to get married?"

Mathilde answered slowly, "It would be an option." She looked at Larry. "Would they kill us?"

Larry laughed. "No. They'll be mad for a while but they probably won't kill us. But you want a big wedding, Mathilde."

She pondered this as Father Phillip finished the job in the sink. "Either way. We'll pray that the Lord opens up the right path for you. And in the meantime, maybe you should say one Our Father together at night and ask God to protect your relationship. We can start tonight. Is that reasonable?"

The couple looked at each other and Father Phillip noted the hope in the young man's face. He prayed.

Mathilde finally spoke, "Yes. We can do that, Larry. Let's do it that way."

Three month's later, after Father Phillip had moved to a new parish, he sat in a coffee shop at lunch time. At the table next to him, two young women passed pictures back and forth. He ignored their conversation until he heard one say to the other, "I always thought Mathilde and Larry would have a huge wedding but they went away with their parents and got married in Rome."

It's Not Personal

Emily's eyes snapped open into the night.

Who was sick?

Her mind caught up with her in a rush and she listened intently to the breathing of her young son who slept beside her. His little six-year-old body lay curled up, nearly in a ball, with one hand clutching his small blanket and the other resting in what appeared to be an impossible angle against his fever-red cheek. Emily gently straightened his hand and felt his forehead. Not too bad. Jonathan was prone to strange viruses and Emily knew the worst had past. This was the third night of spiking fevers and barking coughs. She felt hyper-alert and tried to settle back into sleep as she checked the clock and realized with dismay that only two short hours separated her from another gruelling day.

Last night Jonathan seemed to get worse and in desperation Emily had taken him to the Emergency Room. Hospital personnel treated his breathing and sent them home. She rolled over onto her side and studied her son's face. He looked like his Dad, only smaller. Emily wondered if her husband had been there last night, if she would have taken Jonathan into the hospital. Everything seemed more frightening at night and when one of the children was sick, being alone made it that much more unnerving.

Emily expelled a breath loudly in the silence of her bedroom. She had never wanted to be a single parent. She had never wanted to be divorced. How had she gotten into this situation? She searched again for an answer. How does a husband leave so suddenly after ten years of marriage?

She replayed the end and bitterly scolded herself. It was sudden to her. But one searingly obvious fact confirmed itself day after day and that was that she was the only one surprised when her husband walked out. He had been seeing the woman for months, possibly years. Emily stared at her son's face as if in his resemblance to his father she could find the answers. When did her husband stop loving her? Why? As far as Emily could see, nothing had changed over the years. It was all so busy, she mused. The kids, the work. No red lights had flashed in the kitchen, or the living room or in the garage. There should be a law that a wife gets two years notice when a husband is going to walk out. There should be fights and maybe threats and tears, some tell-tale signs that something is ending that everything else is supposed to be resting on.

One day, she was a married woman in what she thought was a stable relationship. One month later, Emily waved good-bye to her children as they went off with Dad to visit the new house he shared with his…girl friend? Mistress? And now fiancé? It could not be real.

"I can't handle this," Emily thought again as she started to cry quietly in the darkness.

— — — — — — — — — — —

"Are you okay, Mom?" her ten-year-old daughter asked. "Is everything okay?"

Suppressing a wave of irritation, Emily responded cheerfully from the sink. "I'm fine, Jessica, just fine. Finish your cereal and let's get going."

"When is Jonathan going back to school?" Jessica asked.

"Umm, maybe tomorrow, if his fever is down."

Jessica took another bite, thoughtfully. Emily waited. The questions came in packs. "Does Dad know Jonathan is sick? He might want to come home if he thinks Jonathan is sick, Mom. Should you call him?"

Emily disciplined her face. "I think Jonathan will be just fine, Jess. I don't think we need to call Dad."

"Maybe Dad will want to rent him movies, though, Mom. He usually does that when we are sick. He might want to rent him some movies and bring him 7-UP. That's what he always does. Maybe I should call him. He told me to call him if I needed him."

Emily frowned as she tip-toed through this mutually emotional mine field. She would like to say, 'Dad doesn't give a darn or he'd be here' but that would not be consistent with the reassuring tone she aimed for with Jessica. On a good day, Jessica, bright as a button, was a delight. The separation had thrown her into anxious fear that prompted compulsive questions. Emily waged a constant battle against her impatience with her daughter's incessant queries.

"I think we're good, Jess. Maybe when you see Dad this weekend you can tell him about it."

Jessica's pony tails moved ever so slightly upwards as she wrinkled her forehead. "Why does Dad want to be married to Sue and not to you? I mean, what's the difference?"

Emily pretended to consider. "I don't know, Jessica. I…I'm not sure." Dear God, who could handle this? What was the answer? Because Dad is a selfish pig? A narcissist? Could these be the right answers? "I think Dad likes her better, Jessica, and it has nothing to do with you or Jonathan. We both love you and we are both going to take good care of you. It will all work out."

Emily could feel the intensive scrutiny of her daughter. Jessica was an emotions detector and sometimes Emily could pull it off and sometimes she couldn't. She knew she was not pulling it off and sat down, once again, to talk it through.

By the time she dropped Jessica off at school with Jonathan buckled sleeping into the backseat in pajamas, Emily felt like she had been through a brutality challenge. She waved her daughter into school, counting the seconds until she could release her face from the smile that held it hostage. Her daughter went in the doors with a final wave on her worried little face and Emily's own face mercifully cracked into grief.

"Hello," said a bright cheerful voice.

'Oh God,' thought Emily. 'I'll die. I really will.' The idea of having to be appropriate was overwhelming, ridiculous, impossible. She turned to the voice and with profound relief recognized Rose, a woman who, while not close to her, was one she trusted.

"How are you doing?" Rose asked quietly. Their eyes met and locked.

"Rose," Emily said in wonder, "He took her to the place we went on our honeymoon." Both women remained perfectly still, as Emily pondered. Taking a deep breath in, she said, "Fine, to answer your question. I'm doing just great really. It's all good. What could be wrong?"

Rose's face was alert.

Emily, unravelling quickly now, felt tears rolling down her face and she glanced in the rear-view mirror to make sure at least Jonathan would not be traumatized by witnessing this grief. "Rose, I think I hate him. I really do. If I could kill my husband, if I could choose between letting him live and having him killed I cannot say with certainty I would let him live."

Rose opened her mouth to speak then closed it again as Emily looked at her with wide, flowing, puzzled eyes. "He just said, 'I fell in love, Emily. It's not about you. It's not personal'. So, I guess it could be worse. You know, it could be about me. It could be personal. And taking her there? Who does something like that? I mean, who would do that?"

"It's stunning, Emily," Rose finally responded, "Stunning."

Emily nodded, sobbing aloud now through the open window of her car.

"Come and sit in my car," Rose offered. "I'll pull up next to yours and then Jonathan can sleep and we can talk."

Emily, silently crying, could only nod. There was no holding these tears back and she abandoned any effort at trying to offer 'normal'. It seemed Rose was chosen to sweep up the broken glass that was this morning in Emily's head. Emily was at rock bottom.

Rose listened compassionately as Emily sobbed in her front seat. "I just can't take it in, you know? It has been a month and my family is talking about lawyers and selling the house and I'm thinking, 'Sell the house? Where will we live? This is our house.'"

"Can you keep it?" asked Rose.

Emily frowned. "I don't know. He always handled the money. I haven't worked since I was pregnant with Jonathan. Rose, he moved in with this woman. I don't know if they own the house, or it's hers or he's rented it. I don't know anything. Rose, I guess he has to pay…child support or something. I don't really care about the money. I am hoping, in a crazy way, that he'll come back. I know it sounds insane but I don't want a divorce."

"Is he talking about a divorce?" Rose asked gently.

Emily nodded and a fresh wave of crying sounded. "He's already got a lawyer. That's why my family is trying to make me get one. Oh Rose, I really want to crack up but the kids need me. I have to pull myself together."

Rose nodded. "You can handle this, Emily. God will help you."

"God?" Emily snapped bitterly. "No thank you. God has certainly not answered any of my prayers. I have always been good. I'm the only one who never stopped going to Mass in college. I pray with the kids. I've been praying for my husband's business for the last year and all the while he has probably been sleeping with her. No wonder there was less money. This is what God gives me as an answer?"

"Emily," Rose answered, "Don't be confused. God didn't leave you. Your husband did."

Emily stopped crying, considering this. "I never thought of it that way," she said. "I guess I just assumed that when my husband abandoned me, God did too." She closed her eyes for a minute. "Why did I think that? Do you think Jesus is still with me?"

Rose became animated. "Of course He's with you. This shouldn't have happened to you. You are right. But God didn't do this. If you get mad at Him, He'll be less able to help you. I'll pray very hard. And don't worry about Jonathan. This virus is nothing sinister. I'm sure it's the same thing my oldest son used to get. They grow out of it. It's croup. You are doing fine and the kids will be okay. The kids *are* ok."

Emily sighed deeply. "Okay, Rose. Thanks. Say a prayer I can figure out this lawyer thing. I can't believe I'm even talking like this but I don't think I can really trust what my husband says at this point."

Rose, looking serious, agreed. "Given the facts, Emily, I think you have to look out for yourself and the children. But it will work out. You can handle this and it will not always hurt this much."

"Right. I feel better. Like I won't die."

"You won't die. You'll be fine. God is with you."

One year later, Emily pulled into the same parking lot. "Out you go," she said to her children. Jessica and Jonathan gathered their things and scrambled out the door. Emily watched them as they joined the line outside of the school doors. She was conscious of deep and weighted weariness. Her heart ached again. One year into her single life and she had been in two ridiculously shallow flirtations. She felt worse, if anything. She was so tired.

"Hi Rose," she called out, hoping for some conversation.

"Emily, hi," Rose said, waving back. "Give me a second."

Rose waved her own children into the line and wandered over to Emily's car.

"How are things?" Rose asked. "How are the kids doing?"

Emily was always so grateful when Rose asked about the children because Rose, of all people, would actually listen. "They're fine, I think, Rose. But I don't think I'm doing so well."

"You're doing fine, Emily. What's wrong?

Emily's face twisted. "I think God wants me to do better, Rose. I'm going nowhere with this dating thing. I mean, what was I thinking? I got up this morning and I thought, this is just a big distraction from the kids. It's like because my husband was with someone else, I thought I should be, too, and the sooner the better." She glanced in the mirror at her hair color. "Look at this. I've been obsessed with how I look. I'm embarrassed. What do I care how I look? For the first time in my life, I can actually forget about what I look like and just love the kids."

Rose was sympathetic. "Emily, you were figuring yourself out. We all get our hair done."

Emily shook her head. "Yeah, but I spent the last year caring way too much about it. I want to do better."

The women exchanged a look and both felt something powerful, a wash of grace, a presence of something strong and beautiful moving between them. Emily experienced repentance in such a wave that she closed her eyes and lifted her face to the sun. It felt so natural to be talking like this to Rose.

"Emily," Rose said smiling. "You can do this. I have a friend. She's divorced and she's very happy. This is what she said. She hung a picture of Jesus in her living room and she considered herself married to him. That's what you can do. If, you feel drawn to seek an annulment and the Church grants one, Jesus may send another husband. Let Him. But don't look for one. For now, concentrate on the kids and being as holy as you can. That's your offering to the Church and to heaven. Emily, you are such a good mother and God needs you to take care of these kids so they can be close to Him. The kids just want you to be okay. If you do this, God will bless you and everyone around you. You have to worry more about becoming the right person than meeting the right person. My friend is doing so well. She said she really feels God's presence with her."

Emily's face brightened. "I would love to meet her, Rose. That's exactly what I'm feeling, that I should do this with Jesus as my husband and even as Father in the house. I was thinking the very same thing."

"I'll introduce you," Rose promised. "You'll love her, Emily and you'll see how she does it. It's beautiful and it's a beautiful life. This woman is saintly."

"Okay," Emily said firmly. "It's time to change my life. I'm certainly ready." Emily mused for a moment. "You know Rose, it could have been worse when my husband left me."

"How?" Rose asked.

"It could have been personal."

Their loud burst of laughter made the children in line turn. Little Jessica studied her mother's face and, after a moment, smiled happily, too. Emily realized that at this moment, she was finally able to return her daughter's smile with honesty. Truly, she realized, the nightmare was over.

Single Parent Lay Apostles of Jesus Christ the Returning King

Single parents are asked by heaven to provide parenting for their children in circumstances where there is only one parent. In these cases, heaven, if allowed, will assume responsibility in a mystical way for the formation that is absent in the mother or father's place. Heaven takes this commitment seriously and when a family entrusts themselves to God, God protects.

Therefore, if a parent is caring for children by him or herself, he or she must view the situation in truth, which is that they are part of a team providing spiritual formation for their children. This team includes the parent, the faith community, and all of heaven.

Specifically, in the case where a father is parenting children alone, he can view Mary, Queen of Heaven, as his mystical partner and the mother of his children. She will provide a feminine influence for the father so that he can absorb what is necessary from her and allow it to flow into his children. Our Lady must be Queen of the house and mother of all in it.

If a woman is parenting children without a father, she can view Jesus Christ as her mystical partner and the father of her children. Jesus will provide a masculine influence for the mother so that she can absorb what is necessary from Him and allow it to flow into her children. Jesus must be King of the house and father of all in it.

Both our Blessed Mother and Jesus Christ the Returning King must be viewed as having dominion over the family because it is through their influence that the correct family identity will develop. And each family has an identity that is distinct to them. This identity consists of all of the members of the family taken with heaven. In this way, whether there is difficulty or ease, sickness or wellness, poverty or affluence, heaven takes the experiences and stirs them into a pot of grace and what emerges is dignity and functionality. The family develops through time into a unit of mission, that is, a group of people walking through life together, serving each other, loving each other, committed to each other's cause always, and representing God's Kingdom here on earth.

There are many different kinds of families and each family has a distinct call to service. It can feel very frightening and lonely to be parenting alone and yet, with God, there is not only peace, there is ultimate success. God provides all that a child needs.

With this awareness, there is a diminished instinct to compensate in an unhealthy way that can confuse children. Children need to be given the truth that this is their family, it is heaven which has assembled this family and each person is called to love each other and take care of each other in kindness and understanding.

Single parents, God is well aware that He is asking you to assume a great responsibility. He will support this request with all that you need.

For your part, single parent lay apostles, accept responsibility for your children with joy and thanksgiving, aware of the privilege that has been awarded to you and the trust that has been placed in you.

It is clear that what is in our hearts is what will come out from us, regardless of what words we use. Because of this, the great battle for successful parenting must be fought in our heads. Our children will receive the message that we carry in our hearts so we must order our hearts and order our thinking to God's truth.

What is God's truth about our children?

Our children are a gift to the world. God has a beautiful plan for each of them. We are called to help form them and direct their thoughts forward into God's plan. Often in single parent families, there is a temptation to view the family as less than ideal or as second best, a fall back position or a consolation prize type of situation. Parents can be tempted to feel that their children cannot possibly get what they need. But this is defeatist. Jesus, if welcomed, will provide exactly what each child needs to flourish in the way that He needs them to flourish. This is a truth and it is a truth which in no way diminishes another truth which is that in most cases, Jesus desires that children be protected by a man and a woman united in holy Matrimony.

In the case of the single parent family, the parent must make daily acts of trust in the Lord. The holiness of this parent is so important because the protection of the formation of the children relies largely on this holiness. One cannot pick up the slack for another if there is only one so the one must be functioning spiritually to communicate to the children the love that God has for them. There must be a serious commitment to identity as a Catholic family. Children will carry this identity with them if they get it from their home.

The parent must rebuke fear. It is so often seen that Jesus cannot resist trust. When we trust Jesus with our children, He rewards our trust by protecting them even in situations where we would believe it impossible. Yes, when the Lord is invoked as King, the final outcome is always one of triumph. I have seen single parents trust God to a ridiculous degree and to a ridiculous degree, God protects their interests. The parent takes everything with Christ and Christ responds by constant oversight of this little unit of missionary witness.

Be brave and confident, single parent lay apostles! God is with you!

Silence

I am certain that Jesus would want us to view our work as prayer.

If we are in prayer, we are generally not talking. If we are in prayer, we are not doing other things. Which one of us can pray to Jesus, communicating with Him, and at the same time communicate reverently with someone else without being distracted? Such a thing is difficult. What happens, in truth, is that we must ignore one thing and focus on the other. If we are working and talking, we are not concentrating on Jesus and our work is not prayer. We may be failing to accept the graces God allowed for that moment.

There are times when our work requires speech. At those times we should speak and that is our prayer. The difficulty comes with useless talking, pointless communications which then become another distraction offered by God's enemy to take our hearts from the contemplation of Him.

In moments of useless communication when we are not in communion with Jesus, the enemy can come with temptation. Our talk is then subject to a dark influence. Our talk can then become subject to the enemy's plan. In many ways and on many occasions we have furthered the plan of Satan through talking and other forms of communication that are not willed by heaven. Better we be mute than assist Satan in tearing down what the Lord attempts to build.

Many things can happen in useless talking and random communication. Often what happens is destructive gossip.

Before any communication, therefore, we must seek to determine if Jesus wants us to communicate. Is Jesus asking us to make this communication? Many times and probably most times the answer will be 'No'. Jesus needs only the smallest percentage of the communications we make.

"Anne," you will groan, "must we watch every word?"

The answer is "Yes." We should watch every word while we are in holiness school. We must learn how to communicate like heavenly creatures and not like earthly creatures. We are all here to learn how to fit in with heaven. We, as a holy community of believers, are called to take on the mind of Christ and all of His holy saints. We believe or we do not believe. If we believe this, then we must try harder to live this, not only on some days, but on all days and not only with some people, but with all people. We must try to live this not only when we are inclined, but most especially and with the greatest determination, when and where we are not inclined.

Silence can generally be kept during work unless it is absolutely necessary to speak. Examine small talk. It is clear that Satan can enter into our minds and our hearts through useless conversations where two or more attempt to assess and pass judgment on the motives of others. We can hear great charity, it is true, and our hearts become light when we hear this. But we also hear great condemnation and ugly suspicion and our hearts become heavy with worry because in this type of talk we cannot fulfill God's plan because we are resisting God's ways.

Chastity

Chastity means the successful integration of sexuality within the person and thus the inner unity of man in his bodily and spiritual being. Sexuality, in which man's belonging to the bodily and biological world is expressed, becomes personal and truly human when it is integrated into the relationship of one person to another, in the complete and lifelong mutual gift of a man and a woman (Catechism of the Catholic Church 2337).

It is clear that the virtue of chastity is compromised in our society. The catechism says that chastity involves the integrity of the person and I think this is important in this way. Christians must view chastity as something that expresses their Christian integrity, or truthfulness. God's enemy has taken this virtue and distorted it to such a degree that it has been all but obliterated as a goal for much of our society.

Even some married people limit the idea of chastity to perhaps avoiding adultery in the sense of extramarital sexual relationships and forget that, as Christians, they are called to be pure in their thoughts and words and in their entertainment.

Clearly, sexual messages are being sent to people from many angles. One could argue that it is impossible to retain a chaste mind and heart in this time. But that is not true because there are many people who are retaining chastity in their minds and hearts. That is not to say that they are not tempted but that they seek to avoid that which tempts. They are working on chastity, having identified it as a desirable goal. Also, a spirit of chastity is beautiful and has nothing to do with temptation. Temptations may be rife, constantly seeking to draw a person into sin. This, by itself, is not sinister. God, Himself, allows temptation. What is disturbing is when a person professing to be living a Christian life is entertaining lust, not fighting it, but rather living it privately. This greatly offends Jesus. This distortion of sexuality can be viewed by some as a 'man being a man' and thus being predictably tempted, but such thinking confuses acquiescence to licentiousness with ongoing predictable struggle.

Let us assume that there will be sexual temptation. We are called to 'gain mastery' over ourselves and this 'apprenticeship in self-mastery' (Catechism of the Catholic Church 2339) will involve learning and process. Also, there may be some days that are better than others. But if we desire chastity, we must try to limit temptations which lead to occasions of sin. Participating in pastimes such as viewing internet or printed pornography or paying a person to engage in sexual acts cannot be viewed as a

'man being a man' or a woman being 'liberated in her sexuality.'
These things are wrong and sinful, in and of themselves. These
actions should be regretted and confessed. Jesus does not want
these things. Jesus would object to such photographs being taken,
never mind videos being filmed which depict serious and savagely
hurtful actions because of the circumstances around them.

The action of viewing these materials by one's self is simply an
extension of a person having sex with him or her self and as such
these actions become masturbatory in nature.

Now perhaps one makes the argument that these films or pictures
are used to enhance a sex life between a married couple who are
experiencing sexual distress, but some things can never be
acceptable and to think that something pure can be taken from
something impure is an attempt to justify that which cannot be
justified. And if the photographs or films should never have been
taken in the first place, and this action has offended Jesus, how can
the use of them at a later date become a good thing?

"One may never do evil so that good may result from it" (CCC
1756).

The response will be that these things can help a marital
relationship that has grown 'stale' sexually. It is difficult to
entertain this because the overriding thought coming to mind is
that sexual sharing is not a sport that one can become bored with,
nor should it be viewed as competitive and as such something to
be perfected. This is a symptom of a world view and not a
heavenly view. People are to be reverenced, not used for physical
gratification and the plan for sexual sharing between two people
includes respect and love. The sexual sharing that takes place
between two people is the end result of the love between them. It
is not the starting point or the apex of a relationship. On the
contrary, it is rather a culmination of the commitment which
grows through joint service and shared goals. It is consistent with
the Creator's plan and it involves dignity and joy, never
degradation or shame.

Sexual sharing is not meant to be memorialized in any way. It is meant to happen in the Eternal Present, the now, and given as a gift to the Creator in the moment.

In the beginning of most marriages, the physical sexual sharing is new and therefore fresh. It holds great wonder and can create a deep emotional response. This is good. Compare it to a new car.

When one first drives a new car, one can experience wonder and delight if one cares at all about cars. Is the primary function of the car to provide one with wonder and delight? No. The primary function is that of providing one with transportation, taking a person from one place to another and helping a person to arrive at a place where he or she is needed. In marriage, once the honeymoon period passes, the primary functions of sexual sharing remain. These are to assist the couple with preserving unity and provide the Creator with the opportunity to send life.

In the same way, the underlying goal of marital sexual intimacy is not limited to physical gratification but extends to expression of the love that God flows between the two. Someone who is bored with his or her sex life should examine other aspects of the relationship. Arguably, the tenderness that comes from gratitude is what keeps the sexual relationship alive and gives it longevity. A caring and respectful treatment of one person toward another will appoint in him a longing to honor the spouse. The idea that pornography or gimmicks are necessary in the sexual sharing of a couple surely must be perplexing to those who understand love. Surely heaven is thinking, 'They've missed the point. They're using each other again.'

To participate in the degradation of sexual intimacy by watching others perform sexual acts on others or on themselves or on children or animals or whatever it is they are doing, is extending Satan's reign over mankind. We must not think that because we did not film these movies or take these pictures, we will escape judgment for their existence if we are participating by looking at or watching such things. Pornography seems to have become an underground, black Roman circus. And yet, so many good and earnest people have become attached to these things because they can be experienced in such secrecy and are so readily available. Heaven would like this to change.

I would urge those who have become attached to pornographic materials to consider first that all people are God's children. Begin by practicing viewing the people involved in pornography as children of God. These people are someone's daughters, sons, mothers, husbands, brother, sisters. Is this what we would want for our daughters, sons, mothers, husbands, brothers, or sisters? Would we want men and women looking at them in this manner? Would we want men and women masturbating while they watched our family members being used in such a reprehensible and sad manner? Is it possible that this was God's plan for any of these people? Could it be that God wanted them to be treated like this? Does God want us participating in this abuse of personhood?

Consider, dear men and women of God, what pain must have brought each of the people you are watching to a place where they would expose themselves to your gaze while being abused sexually. Is it possible that this is God's plan for you?

We must all understand that there are no separations between heaven and earth. All of heaven is with us in each moment, including the moments when we are participating in these pastimes. How does Jesus feel as He views us looking at Satan's plan for these individuals unfolding in front of us? He must feel very sad, indeed. And yet, He is compassionate. And He forgives. But it hurts Him and I think it hurts Him a lot.

With regard to masturbation, I feel certain that Jesus wants His followers to avoid this. It is clear to me that some will have more difficulty with this than others and that some will have more difficulty at one time in their life than at another time. If the struggle to understand our sexuality is universal, then there must be also some universal truths known.

One should not confuse masturbation with natural sexual events which occur when one is asleep or half asleep. One should avoid occasions of temptation such as watching movies with sexual content or viewing pornography. One should understand that often temptations of this nature can become intensified when one is lonely, anxious, unhappy or fearful. Often a person is seeking to comfort themselves or seeking to calm themselves. It is good to search for the underlying source of such distress when one is experiencing a period of enhanced temptation. It is also good to be understanding with oneself but not so understanding that we treat the masturbatory actions as acceptable, because, over time, this habit can erode the beautiful dignity that Jesus places within us.

The good news is that when a person confesses impure actions, the enemy loses his hold because in these types of actions, more than others, the enemy creates a prison using shame and secrecy as weapons of control. This is the same with any of the sexual sins and includes the abuse of men, women or children being used as prostitutes. Imagine how God views these actions. Imagine His sorrowful countenance when He sees one of His children being used as less than an animal.

What do these actions leave in their wake? Shame, yes, because the child of God realizes that this is not the way his or her sexuality is supposed to be celebrated. Is shame a bad thing? It is a bad thing in the hands of the enemy of dignity, yes, but it can be seen also as a good marker that something is not right. Let's call it a red flashing light. Does one feel good about the actions? Does one feel dignified? Or does one feel used?

Masturbation and incidents of pornography and prostitution burn dignity from a person and leave the person empty because the sexual sharing plan is one of intimacy, safety and gratitude. After such a distortion of the act of sexual sharing, one might be left feeling unloved, empty, alone, undignified and ashamed. Instead of the life-giving act, one is experiencing a selfish act, which detracts from the condition of the person instead of affirming the person. The act intended to be shared has been selfishly experienced in a game of sexual solitaire which punctuates one's isolation instead of piercing it. Who has one just been intimate with? A computer screen? A page of a magazine? Does the screen love you? The page? The fantasy? One is left in the same place only worse because one neither acknowledged nor sought to deal with the underlying incongruence that created the need to numb or soothe in the first place. Habitual masturbation is, after all, a symptom which hints at something else.

We are called to live like citizens of heaven.

For when they rise from the dead, they neither marry, nor are given in marriage, but are like angels in heaven (Mark 12:25).

This verse is so important to the truth of our heavenly existence. In heaven, there will be no boyfriends or girlfriends, husbands or wives. There is no marriage in heaven. However, we can rejoice in the sacramental union that we experienced while we lived on earth. Each person will be free to conduct himself or herself in relationships with others, experiencing intimacy and union that is almost inconceivable to a mind which has not seen heaven. What we think of here as sexual intimacy does not exist in heaven. It is not necessary. And it is pitifully limited to compare one with the other, meaning sexual intimacy to heavenly intimacy.

On earth there are times when through distance or circumstance we are separated from someone we love. This will not be the case in heaven. We will be free to communicate and relate to these people to our heart's content. Again, I repeat the phrase that stayed with me most powerfully after the experiences of heaven, "There are no separations."

Those giving the gift of celibacy to the Church are simply offering this human aspect of their sexuality for the good of God's kingdom and these individuals are, in my opinion, living like citizens of heaven in advance of entering that kingdom. In this sense, I see them as ahead of others.

I can see that many seminarians, priests and religious suspect that if they were married they would not have to struggle with issues of chastity. This is inaccurate. First of all, marriage does not guarantee sexual intimacy on demand. Ask any husband. Or any wife.

Secondly, chastity is an area of spiritual distress for the many married people who have been drawn into a cycle of pornography and masturbation. Many have become stuck in a pattern that leaves them isolated from their inner dignity as well as isolated from their spouse.

Thirdly, in every marriage, there are natural times of refrain which can be temporary or permanent by either necessity or pledge.

Given the culture, a wrong perception must be identified and that is that everyone else is having sex all the time or at least more than us.

With regard to the attachment to pornography and masturbation, this must be treated as any other dangerous habit or addiction.

In the *Heaven Speaks about Addictions* booklet, Saint Barnabas tells us *"It can be difficult to make a decision to step away from your addictions. I understand. The enemy convinces you that you need these things to be happy. And yet, you are not happy. Be honest with yourself for a moment and hear me. You are not at peace if you are attached to something so much that you need it, unless it is God. I am referring generally to things that you are putting in your body, but any habit can become destructive if it takes you from your duties or separates you from purity or holiness....addictions, once they hold you, do not let you go until you make a firm decision to stop completely. Only then can heaven remove their power over you and free your soul. My friend, you object in your heart. You hold this addiction close to you and would like me to be wrong. This alone tells you that there is a problem. I am not wrong. I am looking from the heavenly perspective and I assure you, I am correct when I tell you that Jesus wants to free you.*

When first married, as stated, a married couple is very interested in the physical expression of their sexuality. This is true. But after a short time elapses, the couple must then develop a higher intimacy. They are working closely as a team and must protect the team through communication and good conflict resolution. When these things fail, as they do, the couple relies on God to push past the individuals and protect the Sacrament through heavenly grace. Often, couples experience periods of distress in their relationship where they suffer from what can be called a low marital self-esteem. In other words, they feel that their marriage is not as good as other marriages and they can even wonder if their marriage was a mistake. This is the common cold of the vocation to the married life and should not alarm anyone as if the couple remains together for any duration at all, they will experience this not once, but many times.

What is notable about this experience is what comes next. After a time of both self-examination and examination of the relationship, the couple comes back to each other, with the help of grace, and begins a closer examination of the way they are conducting themselves and what actions, if any, led to the disruption in unity. This is how intimacy grows, not through sexual sharing, but through honest self-appraisal and willingness to take responsibility for mistakes made. The key word is honest and each person in the marriage must feel safe in objecting to behaviors that he or she disagrees with.

Since we are talking about chastity, perhaps it is not too far a digression to discuss sexual integrity in the marriage. At no time should anyone feel pressured to participate in sexual actions that are repugnant to them. If the action is not one that Jesus would bless, in other words, if a person is asking their spouse to participate in pornography and the spouse rightfully objects, the other spouse must be respectful of that decision. To bring this type of 'entertainment' into a sacramental union cannot be helpful. Does a woman want her husband thinking of another woman while he is having sex with her? Does a man want his wife fantasizing about another man while she is having sex with him?

Such a crowded room! There are too many people in this room. I am not saying that married men do not think of other women at times or that married women do not think of other men at times but I cannot believe that this is the way that Jesus wants to help a couple who is struggling. Would it be arousing for a man to watch his daughter being used sexually by another man? Would it be arousing for a woman to watch her son being used sexually by another woman? Clearly not. One would feel sickened. Apostles, we simply must accept that the people participating in pornography are someone's children and, at the very least, or perhaps most, they are children of God.

Returning from the digression, it is clear that for a marriage to last, the couple will have to develop a form of intimacy that is above the physical expression of their sexuality. All successful marriages have done so. In a sacramentally mature marriage, two people relate to each other as committed friends and teammates, fellow travellers seeking holiness.

Those in the single vocation or religious life experience similarly intimate relationships, also. These chaste relationships most closely represent the relationships lived by the saints in heaven, which is everyone's final destination.

In today's society, people are fixating on sexual intercourse to the serious detriment of the bigger picture. This is limited and limiting from a spiritual perspective. This obsession with those things erotic can only be a distortion of God's plan for humanity. Christians are called to be different. One of the ways we are called to be different is by complete rejection of pornography, both in our words and in our actions. We do this by setting an example more than talking and by focusing on what is good in others and not where others are making mistakes.

For example, to tell a young girl who is not your daughter that she is dressed immodestly is not helpful if the whole society is dressed the same way. This is for parents to do first. Mothers help by dressing modestly and fathers help by supporting modesty through what they say and in what they watch or allow to be watched on television.

Others should mostly love the girl and affirm in her what is good.

A holy priest returning home after a long stretch away was very disturbed by the fashions of the day. He said, "I'm talking to my niece. Where do I look?" I replied, "Right into her eyes. Tell her she is beautiful and that God loves her. Whatever you do, avoid the chest area." We laughed, of course, but having custody of the eyes is a habit that must be practiced by holy men. I suspect that, like any habit, it gets easier with time. With so few priests, it could have been damaging for the young girl to have as her only experience of clergy someone who criticized her about how she looked when everyone in the room looked the same way.

I once saw a religious sister publicly reprimanding a young girl for wearing a revealing top. It was terribly shaming. Poor Jesus. Such misrepresentations must hurt Him terribly. The young woman was not wearing anything that stood out in the group around her and to choose her and make a public example of her in mixed company was extraordinarily bad judgment at best and at worst, attention-seeking on the part of the religious. The girls were not taught about modesty that day, but cruelty, and this from what those girls now collectively identify as 'The Church'.

Teaching modesty to young girls is a must, though, and like all dealings with our children, we must be gentle. Young men and women are struggling to manage their sexual selves, after all, and it must be stated that they are at the beginning of what can be an unruly and lifetime study. We do not want them to feel humiliated when they are simply struggling to figure themselves out. Any corrections must be exceedingly gentle and respectful.

With regard to both boys and girls, I believe they are entitled to the truth about their sexuality, most particularly about masturbation. We neither want people to have complexes nor addictions. So we must discuss with our children Church teaching on sexuality. Why is pornography wrong? What do other young people in their geographical area think and how does that thinking hold up against our faith teachings?

These conversations can be difficult but if our children are getting fed a diet of distortion with regard to sexuality then we must try to give them an alternative. When even cartoon characters are sexualized and acting out sexually, we must provide our youth with the truth about purity in relationships.

We will only be able to authentically witness if we are striving for chastity in our own lives.

Conclusion

October 31, 2011

Contemplation of the Crucified Christ enables us to accept our sufferings. As we contemplate Jesus, suffering on the cross, we accept our personal sufferings with him. Suffering comes to us and yet we remain at the foot of the cross like John and Mary. John, the beloved apostle, truly provides us with example. Mary, as Mother of Christ and our Mother, provides us with something more, because truly, on that day when Jesus was crucified in His body, Mary was crucified in her soul. Mary offered her son to the Father, uniting her sufferings to His. Mary was formed and born into humanity to co-redeem mankind and it is for this reason that John Paul II called her the Co-Redemptrix. She had an unrepeatable role to play. No saint can compare to Mary because she was destined to be crucified mystically as her son was crucified physically.

Mary, as the new Eve, stood firmly for all of God's children on that day when she stood firmly for her Son. She accepted the suffering of her Son because she accepted, in totality, God's will for Jesus and she accepted, in totality, God's will for her. As Eve rejected God's will, Mary accepted God's will, immovable for the Father's goals. Mary's comfort must have been that the Father ordained all that occurred before her eyes. The sword which pierced her soul carried the ultimate sorrow. It was finished. The Father's goals had been realized in the commitment unto death of his Son. In a sense, Mary delivered Jesus to Calvary for the Father and also witnessed the plan to its conclusion.

Apostles, we must accept the cross for ourselves and we must accept the crosses God wills for those around us. There is no use railing at the cross. If we rail against the cross we rail against the reality that we are adopted sons and daughters of the Father, sharing in the Sonship of Jesus. When someone we love is crucified, we must provide that person with a holy witness to the anguish as Mary provided Jesus with a holy witness to the anguish. This is what family members do for each other.

Jesus is our example when we are suffering. And Mary is a powerful example for us when someone close to us is suffering or when we are called to minister to any of God's children in their suffering. We study Mary for this reason and for many other reasons, including the following.

Mary was God's choice for the human witness to the life of Jesus. Mary was God's response to Eve. Jesus, it must be noted, retained His divinity even as He claimed His humanity in Mary's womb. Mary had no such divinity. Mary was human. And yet her role in the Church was essential, as opposed to incidental. She carried her suffering in her humanity, it would seem, with the same mystical lights and directives as we receive from time to time to preserve us on our journey. But Mary's participation in the Crucifixion can never be replicated. Her role will never come again.

Jesus wants to live His resurrected life in and through each of us. But in Mary, He also began His human life. She was the tabernacle to the One who would become the Redeemer. Even now, Mary mystically carries Christ, and the body of Mary, as the tabernacle for Christ, has been preserved for eternity.

In heaven, we will have Christ in us. He will possess us and we will possess Him. But only Mary will have had Jesus Christ in her both physically and spiritually. She was the Tabernacle of the Redeemer in both His humanity and His divinity. And it is for this reason that Mary was crucified with her Son, truly and accurately. Because even as God possessed Mary through her Yes answer, she, in a sense, possessed Him by carrying the Savior in her body. The Father created her immaculate for this role. He, as Father, craved a mother for His children, a "Yes" to Eve's "No." In Mary He created the most beautiful complement to His paternity. As Eve said no to the Father, Mary said yes and as Eve drew God's children into the fall, Mary leads God's children into Redemption.

Apostles, we are each called to serve after the example of Mary. The Resurrected Christ wants the gift of redemption He secured for us to be presented to others through our yes answer to Him.

We think of St. Francis and St. Dominic. They, by allowing Christ to work through them, participated powerfully in the redemption of mankind. Indeed, Francis allowed Christ to possess Him so completely that the wounds of the Savior actually opened out and erupted again into the physicality of mankind. We know that periodically God sends these 'big hitters', as it were. Most of us will be smaller versions of this. Can we say that we are less important or that our call to be co-redeemers, or, those who cooperate with Mary and Jesus for mankind is less imperative? No. That is exactly what God's enemy wants us to think, that we are irrelevant, that our yes answer is of no great importance to the Kingdom. On the contrary, the mystery of the Resurrected Christ is that He has a plan for the redemption of our brothers and sisters that includes each one of us.

With regard to intercessory prayer, we are all mediators for humanity, in and through Christ. The key is being 'in Christ'. Mary, blessed among women, is the most beautiful example of what happens when humanity is joined to the divinity, something that God wants for all of us. She is Mediatrix, because her will was completely conformed to Christ, the one Mediator between God and man. As Blessed John Paul II said, Mary is Mediatrix because she uniquely participated in the one mediation of Jesus Christ like no other. She is the best example of what occurs when a human being is joined to God, meaning, when humanity is joined supernaturally to the Son.

We are true sons of God and true sons of Mary, just as Jesus was a true son of God and a true son of Mary. God seeks, through grace, to make us like Him who is fully God and man, Jesus. He does this, as Vatican II taught, through the Sacraments, especially the Eucharist where we eat His body and drink His blood, and through a life of virtue. Think, dear apostles, of the Eucharist as God's way of transforming what is human, more and more, into what is divine. The mystery of the Eucharist is truly the mystery of the plan that we have communion with Christ and with one another. Reception of the Eucharist, with even the barest desire to become like Christ, prompts us into our role of intercessors for humanity.

We receive the body and blood of Christ and our being intuitively begins to plead with God for humanity as advocates. Through our reception of Jesus in the Eucharist, we acknowledge His dignity and we then co-naturally acknowledge the dignity of each adopted son of the Father. Apostles, there is more to all of this than meets the eye so let us be reverent about all that we need to learn.

"...When the Spirit of truth comes He will lead you to the complete truth." (John 16:13)

Apostles, if man looks back across time, which man will say that truth failed to communicate itself, over time, in richer and richer detail?

God is always revealing His truth and in this time, God reveals more of the truth about the role of humanity in the Redemption story by revealing more about Mary's role in the Redemption.

Some fear that man erroneously seeks to exalt Mary above her lowly station, but, dear apostles, it was God, Himself, who exalted Mary. Mary's soul magnifies the Lord and nobody can take that away from us. We need this because we want our soul, also to magnify the Lord. We must accept Mary's example, even as we accept the example of the Firstborn. Only in accepting the truth about Mary will we come to understand the full truth about her Son and the full truth about ourselves. Knowing Christ is our goal and in heaven we will possess our souls with Christ. If we want to move further into knowing the Savior, we will accept Mary's role in receiving Jesus from God in order to deliver Him to each one of us. And this is another point. Mary received the Son from God into her body and delivered Him, not just for that moment in history, not just for the people alive at the first Christmas, but mystically, for all time and for all of God's children. Truly, Mary is the Queen of Apostles and mother to us all.

Mary pleads with Jesus on our behalf, just as she did at Cana when the couple ran out of wine at their wedding feast and this is why she is referred to by the Church in her most ancient title as the

Advocate. She, in an ongoing way, views our impoverishment and goes to her Son, bringing our needs to Him, again and again. We need Jesus. Mary possesses Jesus in a way none of us can or will. She, then, is the one who brings Him to us, over time, through time, and for all time. We bring Jesus to others, it is true, in our shared role as advocates. But none of us does it in the same way that Mary did. Mary is unique and unrepeatable and only through understanding her better will we come to understand more fully the truth about the Trinity.

_._._._._._._._._._._._._

"Baptism not only purifies from all sins, but also makes the neophytes "a new creature," an adopted son of God, who has become a "partaker of the divine nature," member of Christ and co-heir with Him, and a temple of the Holy Spirit" (Catechism of the Catholic Church 1265).

It is true that all Christians are adopted sons of God, co-heirs with Him. In view of this, all Christians deserve the truth that, as adopted sons of God, they are called to cooperation with the Redemption of mankind. Only by coming to a more complete understanding of Mary and her role will they understand the sweetness of their role as followers of her Son. Fuller understanding of Mary's role will unite Christians in their mandate to deliver Jesus to a hurting world, sadly separated from the comfort of the Savior.

Apostles, we must accept the sufferings that come from God. Jesus saw His executioners as agents of the Father's will (*The Wound of Love, A Carthusian Miscellany*). Let it be known that we, along with Mary, accept our share of the sufferings of Christ. When the Crucified One whispers from the cross, may we be there, like Mary, listening intently, fully engaged with the Savior as He prepares to abandon His earthly throne, the Cross, and proceed to His heavenly Throne as King.

For it is when we accept the Returning King and allow Him to flow through us that the renewal will be achieved, giving life to the words of Isaiah, "The people that walked in darkness have seen a great light" (Isaiah 9:1).

Appendix

Guidelines for Lay Apostles

As lay apostles of Jesus Christ the Returning King, we agree to perform our basic obligations as practicing Catholics. Additionally, we will adopt the following spiritual practices, as best we can:

1. **Allegiance Prayer** and **Morning Offering**, plus a brief prayer for the Holy Father
2. **Eucharistic Adoration**, one hour per week
3. **Prayer Group Participation**, monthly, at which we pray the Luminous Mysteries of the Holy Rosary and read the Monthly Message
4. **Monthly Confession**
5. Further, we will follow the example of Jesus Christ as set out in the Holy Scripture, treating all others with His patience and kindness.

Allegiance Prayer

Dear God in Heaven, I pledge my allegiance to You. I give You my life, my work and my heart. In turn, give me the grace of obeying Your every direction to the fullest possible extent. Amen.

Morning Offering

O Jesus, through the Immaculate Heart of Mary, I offer You the prayers, works, joys and sufferings of this day, for all the intentions of Your Sacred Heart, in union with the Holy Sacrifice of the Mass throughout the world, in reparation for my sins, and for the intentions of the Holy Father. Amen.

Prayer for the Holy Father

Blessed Mother of Jesus, protect our Holy Father, Benedict XVI, and bless his intentions.

Five Luminous Mysteries

1. The Baptism of Jesus
2. The Wedding at Cana
3. The Proclamation of the Kingdom of God
4. The Transfiguration
5. The Institution of the Eucharist

Promise from Jesus to His Lay Apostles

May 12, 2005

Your message to souls remains constant. Welcome each soul to the rescue mission. You may assure each lay apostle that just as they concern themselves with My interests, I will concern Myself with theirs. They will be placed in My Sacred Heart and I will defend and protect them. I will also pursue complete conversion of each of their loved ones. So you see, the souls who serve in this rescue mission as My beloved lay apostles will know peace. The world cannot make this promise as only Heaven can bestow peace on a soul. This is truly Heaven's mission and I call every one of Heaven's children to assist Me. You will be well rewarded, My dear ones.

Prayers Taken from The Volumes

Prayers to God the Father

"I trust You, God. I offer You my pain in the spirit of acceptance and I will serve You in every circumstance."

"God my Father in Heaven, You are all mercy. You love me and see my every sin. God, I call on You now as the Merciful Father. Forgive my every sin. Wash away the stains on my soul so that I may once again rest in complete innocence. I trust You, Father in Heaven. I rely on You. I thank You. Amen."

"God my Father, calm my spirit and direct my path."

"God, I have made mistakes. I am sorry. I am Your child, though, and seek to be united to You."

"I believe in God. I believe Jesus is calling me. I believe my Blessed Mother has requested my help. Therefore I am going to pray on this day and every day."

"God my Father, help me to understand."

Prayers to Jesus

"Jesus, I give You my day."

"Jesus, how do You want to use me on this day? You have a willing servant in me, Jesus. Allow me to work for the Kingdom."

"Lord, what can I do today to prepare for Your coming? Direct me, Lord, and I will see to Your wishes."

"Lord, help me."

"Jesus, love me."

Prayers to the Angels

"Angels from Heaven, direct my path."

"Dearest angel guardian, I desire to serve Jesus by remaining at peace. Please obtain for me the graces necessary to maintain His divine peace in my heart."

Prayers for a Struggling Soul

"Jesus, what do You think of all this? Jesus, what do You want me to do for this soul? Jesus, show me how to bring You into this situation."

"Angel guardian, thank you for your constant vigil over this soul. Saints in Heaven, please assist this dear angel."

Prayers for Children

"God in Heaven, You are the Creator of all things. Please send Your graces down upon our world."

"Jesus, I love You."

"Jesus, I trust in You. Jesus, I trust in You. Jesus, I trust in You."

"Jesus, I offer You my day."

"Mother Mary, help me to be good."

How to Recite the Chaplet of Divine Mercy

The Chaplet of Mercy is recited using ordinary Rosary beads of five decades. The Chaplet is preceded by two opening prayers from the *Diary* of Saint Faustina and followed by a closing prayer.

1. Make the Sign of the Cross

In the name of the Father, and of the Son, and of the Holy Spirit. Amen.

2. Optional Opening Prayers

You expired, Jesus, but the source of life gushed forth for souls, and the ocean of mercy opened up for the whole world. O Fount of Life, unfathomable Divine Mercy, envelop the whole world and empty Yourself out upon us.

O Blood and Water, which gushed forth from the Heart of Jesus as a fountain of mercy for us, I trust in You!

3. Our Father

Our Father, who art in Heaven, hallowed be Thy name. Thy Kingdom come. Thy will be done on earth as it is in Heaven. Give us this day our daily bread. And forgive us our trespasses, as we forgive those who trespass against us. And lead us not into temptation, but deliver us from evil. Amen.

4. Hail Mary

Hail Mary, full of grace, the Lord is with thee. Blessed art thou among women, and blessed is the fruit of thy womb, Jesus. Holy Mary, Mother of God, pray for us sinners, now and at the hour of our death. Amen.

5. The Apostles' Creed

I believe in God, the Father Almighty, Creator of Heaven and earth. I believe in Jesus Christ, His only Son, Our Lord. He was conceived by the power of the Holy Spirit and born of the Virgin Mary. He suffered under Pontius Pilate, was crucified, died, and was buried. He descended to the dead. On the third day He rose again. He ascended into Heaven, and is seated at the right hand of the Father. He will come again to judge the living and the dead. I believe in the Holy Spirit, the holy Catholic Church, the Communion of Saints, the forgiveness of sins, the resurrection of the body, and life everlasting. Amen.

6. The Eternal Father

Eternal Father, I offer You the Body and Blood, Soul and Divinity of Your Dearly Beloved Son, our Lord, Jesus Christ, in atonement for our sins and those of the whole world.

7. On the Ten Small Beads of Each Decade

For the sake of His Sorrowful Passion, have mercy on us and on the whole world.

8. Repeat for the remaining decades

Saying the "Eternal Father" (6) on the "Our Father" bead and then 10 "For the sake of His Sorrowful Passion" (7) on the following "Hail Mary" beads.

9. Conclude with Holy God

Holy God, Holy Mighty One, Holy Immortal One, have mercy on us and on the whole world.

10. Optional Closing Prayer

Eternal God, in whom mercy is endless and the treasury of compassion—inexhaustible, look kindly upon us and increase Your mercy in us, that in difficult moments we might not despair nor become despondent, but with great confidence submit ourselves to Your holy will, which is Love and Mercy itself.

To learn more about the image of The Divine Mercy, the Chaplet of Divine Mercy and the series of revelations given to St. Faustina Kowalska please contact:

Marians of the Immaculate Conception
Stockbridge, Massachusetts 01263
Telephone 800-462-7426
www.marian.org

How to Pray the Rosary

1. Make the Sign of the Cross and say the "Apostles Creed."
2. Say the "Our Father."
3. Say three "Hail Marys."
4. Say the "Glory be to the Father."
5. Announce the First Mystery; then say the "Our Father."
6. Say ten "Hail Marys," while meditating on the Mystery.
7. Say the "Glory be to the Father." After each decade say the following prayer requested by the Blessed Virgin Mary at Fatima: "O my Jesus, forgive us our sins, save us from the fires of hell, lead all souls to Heaven, especially those in most need of Thy mercy."
8. Announce the Second Mystery: then say the "Our Father." Repeat 6 and 7 and continue with the Third, Fourth, and Fifth Mysteries in the same manner.
9. Say the "Hail, Holy Queen" on the medal after the five decades are completed.

As a general rule, depending on the season, the Joyful Mysteries are said on Monday and Saturday; the Sorrowful Mysteries on Tuesday and Friday; the Glorious Mysteries on Wednesday and Sunday; and the Luminous Mysteries on Thursday.

Papal Reflections of the Mysteries

The Joyful Mysteries

The Joyful Mysteries are marked by the joy radiating from the event of the Incarnation. This is clear from the very first mystery, the Annunciation, where Gabriel's greeting to the Virgin of Nazareth is linked to an invitation to messianic joy: "Rejoice, Mary." The whole of salvation... had led up to this greeting.

(Prayed on Mondays and Saturdays, and optional on Sundays during Advent and the Christmas Season.)

The Luminous Mysteries

Moving on from the infancy and the hidden life in Nazareth to the public life of Jesus, our contemplation brings us to those mysteries which may be called in a special way "mysteries of light." Certainly, the whole mystery of Christ is a mystery of light. He is the "Light of the world" (John 8:12). Yet this truth emerges in a special way during the years of His public life. (Prayed on Thursdays.)

The Sorrowful Mysteries

The Gospels give great prominence to the Sorrowful Mysteries of Christ. From the beginning, Christian piety, especially during the Lenten devotion of the Way of the Cross, has focused on the individual moments of the Passion, realizing that here is found the culmination of the revelation of God's love and the source of our salvation. (Prayed on Tuesdays and Fridays, and optional on Sundays during Lent.)

The Glorious Mysteries

"The contemplation of Christ's face cannot stop at the image of the Crucified One. He is the Risen One!" The Rosary has always expressed this knowledge born of faith and invited the believer to pass beyond the darkness of the Passion in order to gaze upon Christ's glory in the Resurrection and Ascension... Mary herself would be raised to that same glory in the Assumption. (Prayed on Wednesdays and Sundays.)

From the *Apostolic Letter The Rosary of the Virgin Mary*, Pope John Paul II, Oct. 16, 2002.

Prayers of the Rosary

The Sign of the Cross

In the name of the Father, and of the Son, and of the Holy Spirit. Amen.

The Apostles' Creed

I believe in God, the Father Almighty, Creator of Heaven and earth. I believe in Jesus Christ, His only Son, Our Lord. He was conceived by the power of the Holy Spirit and born of the Virgin Mary. He suffered under Pontius Pilate, was crucified, died, and was buried. He descended to the dead. On the third day He rose again. He ascended into Heaven, and is seated at the right hand of the Father. He will come again to judge the living and the dead. I believe in the Holy Spirit, the holy Catholic Church, the Communion of Saints, the forgiveness of sins, the resurrection of the body, and life everlasting. Amen.

Our Father

Our Father, who art in Heaven, hallowed be Thy name. Thy Kingdom come. Thy will be done on earth as it is in Heaven. Give us this day our daily bread. And forgive us our trespasses, as we forgive those who trespass against us. And lead us not into temptation, but deliver us from evil. Amen.

Hail Mary

Hail Mary, full of grace, the Lord is with thee. Blessed art thou among women, and blessed is the fruit of thy womb, Jesus. Holy Mary, Mother of God, pray for us sinners, now and at the hour of our death. Amen.

Glory Be to the Father

Glory be to the Father, and to the Son, and to the Holy Spirit. As it was in the beginning, is now, and ever shall be, world without end. Amen.

Hail Holy Queen

Hail, Holy Queen, Mother of Mercy, our life, our sweetness and our hope. To thee do we cry, poor banished children of Eve. To thee do we send up our sighs, mourning and weeping in this valley of tears. Turn then, most gracious Advocate, thine eyes of mercy towards us. And after this, our exile, show unto us the blessed fruit of thy womb, Jesus. O clement, O loving, O sweet Virgin Mary!

Pray for us, O Holy Mother of God.
That we may be made worthy of the promises of Christ.

The Mysteries

First Joyful Mystery:
The Annunciation

And when the angel had come to her, he said, "Hail, full of grace, the Lord is with thee. Blessed art thou among women."

(Luke 1:28)

One Our Father, Ten Hail Marys,
One Glory Be, etc.

Fruit of the Mystery: ***Humility***

Second Joyful Mystery:
The Visitation

Elizabeth was filled with the Holy Spirit and cried out in a loud voice: "Blest are you among women and blest is the fruit of your womb." (Luke 1:41-42)

One Our Father, Ten Hail Marys,
One Glory Be, etc.

Fruit of the Mystery: ***Love of Neighbor***

Third Joyful Mystery:
The Birth of Jesus

She gave birth to her first-born Son and wrapped Him in swaddling clothes and laid Him in a manger, because there was no room for them in the place where travelers lodged.   (*Luke* 2:7)
One *Our Father*, Ten *Hail Marys*,
One *Glory Be*, etc.
Fruit of the Mystery: ***Poverty***

Fourth Joyful Mystery:
The Presentation

When the day came to purify them according to the law of Moses, the couple brought Him up to Jerusalem so that He could be presented to the Lord, for it is written in the law of the Lord, "Every first-born male shall be consecrated to the Lord."
(*Luke* 2:22-23)
One *Our Father*, Ten *Hail Marys*,
One *Glory Be*, etc.
Fruit of the Mystery: ***Obedience***

Fifth Joyful Mystery:
The Finding of the Child Jesus in the Temple

On the third day they came upon Him in the temple sitting in the midst of the teachers, listening to them and asking them questions.   (*Luke* 2:46)
One *Our Father*, Ten *Hail Marys*,
One *Glory Be*, etc.
Fruit of the Mystery: ***Joy in Finding Jesus***

First Luminous Mystery:
The Baptism of Jesus

And when Jesus was baptized… the heavens were opened and He saw the Spirit of God descending like a dove, and alighting on Him, and lo, a voice from Heaven, saying "this is My beloved Son," with whom I am well pleased."   (*Matthew* 3:16-17)
One *Our Father*, Ten *Hail Marys*,
One *Glory Be*, etc.
Fruit of the Mystery: ***Openness to the Holy Spirit***

Second Luminous Mystery:
The Wedding at Cana

His mother said to the servants, "Do whatever He tells you." . . .
Jesus said to them, "Fill the jars with water." And they filled them
up to the brim.

(John 2:5-7)

One *Our Father*, Ten *Hail Marys*,
One *Glory Be*, etc.

Fruit of the Mystery: ***To Jesus through Mary***

Third Luminous Mystery:
The Proclamation of the Kingdom of God

"And preach as you go, saying, 'The Kingdom of Heaven is at
hand.' Heal the sick, raise the dead, cleanse lepers, cast out
demons. You received without pay, give without pay."

(Matthew 10:7-8)

One *Our Father*, Ten *Hail Marys*,
One *Glory Be*, etc.

Fruit of the Mystery: ***Repentance and Trust in God***

Fourth Luminous Mystery:
The Transfiguration

And as He was praying, the appearance of His countenance was
altered and His raiment become dazzling white. And a voice came
out of the cloud saying, "This is My Son, My chosen; listen to Him!"

(Luke 9:29, 35)

One *Our Father*, Ten *Hail Marys*,
One *Glory Be*, etc.

Fruit of the Mystery: ***Desire for Holiness***

Fifth Luminous Mystery:
The Institution of the Eucharist

And He took bread, and when He had given thanks He broke it and gave it to them, saying, "This is My body which is given for you." . . . And likewise the cup after supper, saying, "This cup which is poured out for you is the new covenant in My blood."

(*Luke* 22:19-20)

One *Our Father*, Ten *Hail Marys*,
One *Glory Be*, etc.

Fruit of the Mystery: **Adoration**

First Sorrowful Mystery:
The Agony in the Garden

In His anguish He prayed with all the greater intensity, and His sweat became like drops of blood falling to the ground. Then He rose from prayer and came to His disciples, only to find them asleep, exhausted with grief.   (*Luke* 22:44-45)

One *Our Father*, Ten *Hail Marys*,
One *Glory Be*, etc.

Fruit of the Mystery: **Sorrow for Sin**

Second Sorrowful Mystery:
The Scourging at the Pillar

Pilate's next move was to take Jesus and have Him scourged.

(*John* 19:1)

One *Our Father*, Ten *Hail Marys*,
One *Glory Be*, etc.

Fruit of the Mystery: **Purity**

Third Sorrowful Mystery:
The Crowning with Thorns

They stripped off His clothes and wrapped Him in a scarlet military cloak. Weaving a crown out of thorns they fixed it on His head, and stuck a reed in His right hand...   (*Matthew* 27:28-29)

One *Our Father*, Ten *Hail Marys*,
One *Glory Be*, etc.

Fruit of the Mystery: **Courage**

Fourth Sorrowful Mystery:
The Carrying of the Cross

... carrying the cross by Himself, He went out to what is called
the Place of the Skull (in Hebrew, Golgotha).   (*John* 19:17)
One *Our Father*, Ten *Hail Marys*,
One *Glory Be*, etc.
Fruit of the Mystery: ***Patience***

Fifth Sorrowful Mystery:
The Crucifixion

Jesus uttered a loud cry and said, "Father, into Your hands I
commend My spirit." After He said this, He expired. (*Luke* 23:46)
One *Our Father*, Ten *Hail Marys*,
One *Glory Be*, etc.
Fruit of the Mystery: ***Perseverance***

First Glorious Mystery:
The Resurrection

You need not be amazed! You are looking for Jesus of Nazareth,
the one who was crucified. He has been raised up; He is not here.
See the place where they laid Him."   (*Mark* 16:6)
One *Our Father*, Ten *Hail Marys*,
One *Glory Be*, etc.
Fruit of the Mystery: ***Faith***

Second Glorious Mystery:
The Ascension

Then, after speaking to them, the Lord Jesus was taken up into
Heaven and took His seat at God's right hand.   (*Mark* 16:19)
One *Our Father*, Ten *Hail Marys*,
One *Glory Be*, etc.
Fruit of the Mystery: ***Hope***

Third Glorious Mystery:
The Descent of the Holy Spirit

All were filled with the Holy Spirit. They began to express themselves in foreign tongues and make bold proclamation as the Spirit prompted them. *(Acts* 2:4)

One *Our Father*, Ten *Hail Marys*,
One *Glory Be*, etc.

Fruit of the Mystery: ***Love of God***

Fourth Glorious Mystery:
The Assumption

You are the glory of Jerusalem… you are the splendid boast of our people… God is pleased with what you have wrought. May you be blessed by the Lord Almighty forever and ever.

(Judith 15:9-10)

One *Our Father*, Ten *Hail Marys*,
One *Glory Be*, etc.

Fruit of the Mystery: ***Grace of a Happy Death***

Fifth Glorious Mystery:
The Coronation

A great sign appeared in the sky, a woman clothed with the sun, with the moon under her feet, and on her head a crown of twelve stars. *(Revelation* 12:1)

One *Our Father*, Ten *Hail Marys*,
One *Glory Be*, etc.

Fruit of the Mystery: ***Trust in Mary's Intercession***

The Volumes

Direction for Our Times
as given to Anne, a lay apostle

Volume One: ***Thoughts on Spirituality***
Volume Two: ***Conversations with the***
                 Eucharistic Heart of Jesus
Volume Three: ***God the Father Speaks to***
                 His Children
                 The Blessed Mother Speaks
                 to Her Bishops and Priests
Volume Four: ***Jesus the King***
                 Heaven Speaks to Priests
                 Jesus Speaks to Sinners
Volume Six: ***Heaven Speaks to Families***
Volume Seven: ***Greetings from Heaven***
Volume Nine: ***Angels***
Volume Ten: ***Jesus Speaks to His Apostles***

Volumes 5 and 8 will be printed at a later date.

The Volumes are now available in PDF format
for free download and printing from our website:
www.directionforourtimes.org.
We encourage everyone to print and distribute them.

The Volumes are also available at your local bookstore.

The "Heaven Speaks" Booklets
Direction for Our Times
as given to Anne, a lay apostle

The following booklets are available individually from Direction for Our Times:

Heaven Speaks About Abortion
Heaven Speaks About Addictions
Heaven Speaks to Victims of Clerical Abuse
Heaven Speaks to Consecrated Souls
Heaven Speaks About Depression
Heaven Speaks About Divorce
Heaven Speaks to Prisoners
Heaven Speaks to Soldiers
Heaven Speaks About Stress
Heaven Speaks to Young Adults

Heaven Speaks to Those Away from the Church
Heaven Speaks to Those Considering Suicide
Heaven Speaks to Those Who Do Not Know Jesus
Heaven Speaks to Those Who Are Dying
Heaven Speaks to Those Who Experience Tragedy
Heaven Speaks to Those Who Fear Purgatory
Heaven Speaks to Those Who Have Rejected God
Heaven Speaks to Those Who Struggle to Forgive
Heaven Speaks to Those Who Suffer from Financial Need
Heaven Speaks to Parents Who Worry About
   Their Children's Salvation

All twenty of the "Heaven Speaks" booklets are now available for free download and printing from our website www.directionforourtimes.org. We encourage everyone to print and distribute these booklets.

Other Written Works by Anne, a lay apostle

Climbing the Mountain

This book contains the fascinating story of how the rescue mission began and how it has blossomed into a worldwide apostolate under the watchful eye and in complete obedience to the Church. It is the story of The Lay Apostolate of Jesus Christ the Returning King.

Also featured is a summary of Anne's mystical experiences of Heaven. She describes the heavenly home that has been created for God's children. Reading these accounts, you will learn that in Heaven we will experience constant unity with Jesus. Anne also confirms that souls in Heaven work together to assist in answering the prayers of God's earthly children. At one point in time Jesus tells Anne, *"...you are a child of God and you have every right to be here."*

In the section entitled "Climbing the Mountain," Anne writes about her vision of the personal call to holiness that we all must hear.

It concludes with a reprint of the first ten "Heaven Speaks" booklets: Abortion, Addictions, Victims of Clerical Abuse, Consecrated Souls, Depression, Divorce, Prisoners, Soldiers, Stress, and Young Adults.

This is a book to be treasured as it reveals the intimate love of the Savior for each soul. Every reader will be called to great rejoicing, for truly, God's Kingdom comes.

The Mist of Mercy

Anne begins this book by telling us that the enemy of God is present on earth and a battle is being waged for souls. Satan is trying to destroy God's plan for us, which is unity with Him in Heaven for eternity. We must be alert to these efforts and be armed for the battle. This is the reality of spiritual warfare.

Following is a section entitled *Snapshots of Reality* which is a collection of short stories depicting realistic earthly struggles while including a glimpse of these same situations from the heavenly perspective and how our friends, the saints, act on our behalf more than we can imagine.

Also in this book is Anne's account of her mystical experiences of Purgatory. She tells us of the souls she saw there and describes the prayers they prayed and the remorse they felt for the choices they had made on earth which were against the will of God. You will be happy to learn that Purgatory is a great mercy of God and allows each soul there the perfect experience of preparation for eternity in Heaven.

The last section is a reprint of the Monthly Messages from Jesus Christ dated from December 1, 2004 through June 1, 2006.

Serving in Clarity

This book could be described as the guidebook for lay apostles who wish to serve Jesus Christ the Returning King. In essence, it is the walking guide, given to us by Heaven, describing how to obtain clarity so that our path up the Mountain of Holiness can be clearly identified.

The writing includes locutions from Jesus and Mary, encouraging us to trust that Heaven is sending extraordinary graces so that we will say "yes" to helping Jesus usher in the Age of Obedience.

Anne then shares her insight on how we should live our lives in love, holiness and obedience to the Church. Also included are vignettes of real life challenges that priests and people faced while serving in their vocations.

Especially compelling is the description of Anne's mystical experiences of the Mountain of Holiness, where Jesus showed her the current condition of the world so that lay apostles would be encouraged to participate in God's rescue mission for souls.

Reprinted in this book is *In Defense of Obedience and Reflections on the Priesthood,* as well as the Monthly Messages from Jesus dated July 26 through June 2008.

Serving in Clarity is a gift for all those who are serious about learning God's will for their life.

Lessons in Love

Lessons in Love highlights the importance of loving others with the unconditional love that Jesus has for each one of us. Anne illuminates a hopeful path of loving the people Jesus has placed in our lives. In particular, she shares her thoughts on the sacramental call to marriage and offers points for consideration when choosing a mate. She gives suggestions to navigate predictable marital difficulties and challenges. Also included is a series of thoughts for those living with homosexuality.

We learn about the place of the divine will. We read about the fruits of the renewal in which we are all asked to participate. Anne discuses some frequently asked questions regarding our Catholic faith, guiding us in our interactions with non-Christians. The book concludes with a reprint of five "Heaven Speaks" booklets.

Includes:
- The Place of the Divine Will
- Visions
- God is Love
- Marriage
- Questions and Answers
- Intimacy
- "Heaven Speaks" Booklets

In Defense of Obedience
and
Reflections on the Priesthood

This work by Anne consists of two essays on topics close to the heart of Jesus. The first is entitled *In Defense of Obedience* and the second is entitled *Reflections on the Priesthood*.

In Defense of Obedience is a serious call to return to a spirit of obedience to the Magisterium of the Church. Obedience to the Church is a must for every apostle, laity and clergy alike.

Anne's essay on the priesthood gives us the smallest glimpse of the love our Lord has for the men who hear and answer His call. We read the depth of the connection Jesus has with these men and how they are united in a most unique way to the Sacred Heart of Jesus and the Immaculate Heart of Mary. This is also a gentle reminder that we are called to love and support our priests who serve us in their humanity but with a heavenly dignity bestowed upon them from heaven by Jesus Christ, the First Priest.

This book is part of a non-profit mission.
Our Lord has requested that we
spread these words internationally.

Please help us.

If you would like to assist us financially,
please send your tax-deductible contribution
to the address below:

Direction for Our Times
9000 West 81st Street
Justice, Illinois 60458

www.directionforourtimes.org

Email: contactus@directionforourtimes.com
Phone: 708-496-9300

Direction for Our Times Ireland
The Hague Building
Cullies
Cavan
County Cavan
Ireland

www.directionforourtimes.org

Email: contactus@dfot.ie
Phone: 353-(0)49-437-3040

Direction for Our Times is a 501(c)(3)
not-for-profit corporation. Contributions are
deductible to the extent provided by law.

Jesus gives Anne a message for the world on
the first of each month. To receive the
monthly messages you may access our
website at www.directionforourtimes.org
or call us at 708-496-9300
to be placed on our mailing list.